Socio-economic studies   15

```
LB          Chinapah, Vinayagum.
2822.75
.C5         Evaluating
1990          educational
              programmes and
              projects.
```

$25.00

SOCIAL SCIENCES DIVISION
CHICAGO PUBLIC LIBRARY
400 SOUTH STATE STREET
CHICAGO, IL 60605

BAKER & TAYLOR BOOKS

Currently available in this series:

1. *Evaluating social action projects: principles, methodological aspects and selected examples.*

2. *Socio-economic indicators for planning methodological aspects and selected examples.*

3. *Women and development: indicators of their changing role.*

4. *Planning methods and the human environment.*

5. *Quality of life: problems of assessment and measurement.*

6. *Evaluation manual.*

7. *Applicability of indicators of socio-economic change for development planning.*

8. *Social science methods, decision-making and development planning.*

10. *Evaluation in Latin America and the Caribbean: selected experiences. (Also published in Spanish.)*

11. *Planning integrated development: methods used in Asia.*

12. *Socio-economic analysis and planning: critical choice of methodologies.*

13. *Women's issues in development planning.*

14. *Innovative approaches to development planning.*

15. *Evaluating educational programmes and projects: holistic and practical considerations.*

Evaluating educational programmes and projects: holistic and practical considerations

*Vinayagum Chinapah
and Gary Miron*

Unesco

The authors are responsible for the choice
and the presentation of the facts contained
in this book and for the opinions expressed
therein, which are not necessarily those of
Unesco and do not commit the Organization.

Published in 1990 by the United Nations Educational,
Scientific and Cultural Organization
7 place de Fontenoy, 75700 Paris
Printed by Duculot, Gembloux (Belgium)

ISBN 92-3-102648-8

© Unesco 1990
Printed in Belgium

Preface

The present volume, fifteenth in the series "*Socio-economic Studies*", is devoted to approaches, designs and techniques for evaluating educational programmes and projects, a subject which is increasingly being recognized as an integral part of policy-making and of the implementation of programmes and projects.

The potential contribution of evaluation to improving both the planning and execution of programmes and projects and to a better utilization of resources, directing them to the desired beneficiaries, is now well recognized. Indeed, evaluation is a permanent concern both for those who determine the major orientations of social and economic policies and for those who are charged with their implementation. In this sense, evaluation can be considered, in the process of planned development, as one side of a triangle, of which the other two sides are formulation of programmes and projects, and their implementation.

The present volume, "*Evaluating Educational Programmes and Projects: Holistic and Practical Considerations*", has been prepared by Vinayagum Chinapah, Deputy Director and Associate Professor, and Gary Miron, Research Assistant, both of the Institute of International Education, University of Stockholm.

The volume is divided into three integrated and mutually dependent parts. In Part One, which is divided into three sections, some major theoretical, methodological and operational issues in evaluation, in particular educational evaluation, are discussed. In Part Two, the real and practical world of educational evaluation is examined. It focuses on some important principles and practices in the evaluation of various educational areas, i.e. primary education (Chapter 2), literacy (Chapter 3) and technical/vocational education (Chapter 4).

Part Three of this volume is considered by the authors as the core of the entire work, as it attempts to bridge the gap between theoretical and methodological prescriptions for educational evaluation and its practice. Three concrete practical experiences in educational evaluation, all from developing countries, are presented, drawing upon the theoretical and methodological considerations presented in Parts One and Two. All three experiences highlight the importance of capacity-building in educational evaluation in developing countries.

The final section "Conclusions and Major Recommendations", highlights some of the major conclusions of the work. Recommendations are made which largely address the issues of educational evaluation in developing countries, and strategies for capacity-building are presented.

Comments and suggestions about this issue, and the series in general, as well as requests for copies of this and past issues may be addressed to the Division of Studies for Development, Unesco, 7, place de Fontenoy, 75700 Paris, France.

Contents

List of figures and tables 11
Acknowledgements 13
Abbreviations 14
Summary 15

PART ONE

THEORETICAL, METHODOLOGICAL AND OPERATIONAL ISSUES

Introduction 23

1. Evaluation: an overview

    1.1 The theoretical framework for evaluation 26
    1.2 Methodological considerations 37
    1.3 Operational issues 50

PART TWO

EVALUATING SPECIFIC AREAS OF EDUCATION

Introduction 59

2. The evaluation of primary education programmes

    2.1 Analysis of aims and objectives of primary education 61
    2.2 Evaluating primary education 66
    2.3 Evaluation designs for primary education 68
    2.4 Major parameters of primary education evaluation: sampling procedures, evaluation instruments and data management 72

3. The evaluation of literacy programmes

    3.1 Aims and objectives of literacy programmes   78
    3.2 Scope and coverage   81
    3.3 The evaluation objectives   83
    3.4 Choice of evaluation designs   84
    3.5 Choice of indicators and variables   86
    3.6 Data-collection procedures and data analysis   88

4. The evaluation of technical/vocational education

    4.1 Aims and objectives of technical/vocational
         education   90
    4.2 The programme setting   92
    4.3 The evaluation setting   94
    4.4 Evaluating the programme content   98
    4.5 Evaluating logistical components   101
    4.6 Evaluating personnel components   102
    4.7 Evaluating programme performance   103

PART THREE

EXPERIENCES IN EDUCATIONAL EVALUATION

Introduction   109

5. The National Educational Evaluation Study of
    Primary Education in Mauritius

    5.1 Basic evaluation questions at the primary
         education level   113
    5.2 The national setting of the evaluation study   114
    5.3 Why primary education?   116
    5.4 Theoretical framework   117
    5.5 Methodological approach   118
    5.6 Evaluation instruments and data base   122
    5.7 Data Collection and data processing   124
    5.8 Structure of analysis   126

6. The Ethiopian Literacy Campaign Evaluation

    6.1 Background to the Ethiopian Literacy Campaign   128
    6.2 Organization and structure of the evaluation
         activity   130
    6.3 Evaluation design and coverage   134
    6.4 Evaluation instruments   135
    6.5 Target population and sampling procedures   138
    6.6 Data collection   139
    6.7 Analytical strategy   142

7. The Evaluation Study of Industrial Education in
   Academic Secondary Schools in Kenya

7.1	The Industrial Education project in Kenya	149
7.2	Background to the evaluation study	151
7.3	Evaluation design and sampling procedures	153
7.4	Evaluation of the project content	155
7.5	Evaluation of the logistical components	156
7.6	Evaluation of the personnel components	158
7.7	Evaluation of the project performance	161

Conclusions and major recommendations

General conclusions	167
Building evaluation capacity in developing countries	170

Bibliography 179

List of figures and tables

FIGURES

1. A comprehensive approach to educational evaluation — 17
2. Ten basic questions in planning evaluation — 32
3. Interplay among frame factors and their components — 35
4. Influences on key actors in the evaluation-decision system — 55
5. A conceptual model of school learning — 119
6. The organization of the ELCE project — 134
7. The conceptual model of the ELCE project (phase I) — 143
8. Analytical model of the ELCE project (phase II) — 144

TABLES

1. Basic paradigms in educational evaluation — 46
2. Nepal: major objectives of primary education — 66
3. Quality control of implemented curriculum over time — 69
4. Description of four probability samples — 74
5. Holistic considerations for data collection — 97
6. Factors and indicators to be considered in the evaluation of equality of access and opportunity to technical/vocational education — 104
7. Basic data for estimating unit cost for technical/vocational education — 106
8. Model for the evaluation study — 158
9. Utilization of workshop capacity — 156

Acknowledgements

This book on educational evaluation has been commissioned by Unesco and prepared by Vinayagum Chinapah, Deputy Director and Associate Professor, and Gary Miron, Research Assistant, both of the Institute of International Education, University of Stockholm, Sweden. The authors would like to thank Unesco for advice and support in the planning and writing of the manuscript. Further recognition and thanks go to Holger Daun for his contribution to Chapters 4 and 7 and to Jan-Åke Engström and Zhao Shangwu for help in preparing the major figures and tables in the book. Both are from the Institute of International Education, University of Stockholm. Finally, the authors wish to express their gratitude to the many individuals who reviewed and provided feedback on the final draft of this work, particularly Torsten Husén, Sixten Marklund and T. Neville Postlethwaite.

Abbreviations

ARNEC	All Round National Education Committee
CERID	Centre for Educational Research Innovation and Development
CPE	Certificate of Primary Education
CPM	Critical Path Method
CSO	Central Statistics Office
ELCE	Ethiopian Literacy Campaign Evaluation
EPF	Educational Production Function
EWLP	Experimental World Literacy Programme
FRA	Field Research Assistant
GTU	Government Teachers' Union
IBE	International Bureau of Education
IDRC	International Development Research Centre
IE	Industrial Education
IEA	International Association for the Evaluation of Educational Achievement
IIE	Institute of International Education
IIEP	International Institute for Educational Planning
JSE	Junior Scholarship Examination
KCE	Kenya Certificate of Education
KS	Kenya-Sweden Technical and Industrial Education project
KSTC	Kenya Science Teacher College
LDC	Least Developed Country
LCCEC	Literacy Campaign Co-ordinating and Executive Committee
LISREL	Linear Structural Relationships
MECA	Ministry of Education and Cultural Affairs
MIE	Mauritian Institute of Education
MIS	Management Information System
NLCCC	National Literacy Campaign Co-ordinating Committee
NNEPC	Nepal National Education Planning Commission
OECD	Organisation for Economic Co-operation and Development
PERT	Programme Evaluation and Review Technique
PLS	Partial Least Squares
PPBS	Planning-Programming-Budgeting System
PSLC	Primary School Leaving Certificate
SAS	Statistical Analysis System
SIDA	Swedish International Development Authority
SPSS	Statistical Package for the Social Sciences
TSS	Technical Secondary Schools
UNDP	United Nations Development Programme

Summary

The main thesis of this work is that evaluation, when confined to programmes of social intervention, and to education in particular, must be properly designed, opportunely organized and effectively implemented. In order to accomplish this, practical experiences must be taken into consideration. Further, as advocated in this book, a holistic approach to evaluation should prove the most effective in overcoming the many barriers that present themselves when evaluation is brought from the planning room to the field.

Although there are increasingly concerted efforts among policy-makers, programme administrators, front-line implementors and target beneficiaries to institutionalize educational evaluation, the support is minimal at present. A great deal of the innovation and improvement in educational evaluation remains a by-product of the works of scholars and researchers in the developed and affluent nations. Lacunae in the field of educational evaluation in developing countries are partly due to the poor capacity to examine critically the progress achieved elsewhere in the field with a view to building up their own capacity tailored to their specific contexts, needs and aspirations. Instead, the choice is often that of espousing evaluation models, approaches, designs, instruments, and so on, developed in the industrialized countries which are considered to be the "most legitimate or easiest route".

This book focuses on three important educational areas: primary education, literacy and technical/vocational education. Emphasis has been given to the linkages between the theory and practice of educational evaluation. This work has attempted to avoid being a replication of textbooks or handbooks of educational evaluation where theory is generally divorced from practice. Some of the experiences accrued in the evaluation of three educational areas in developing countries are considered. Emphasis has been put on a step-by-step description, presentation and examination of these three educational evaluations. Here, the overriding aim is to provide an overview of practical evaluation experiences in the context of developing countries where many of the so-called "theories, paradigms or models of educational evaluation" developed elsewhere become too remote from their intended application.

This work is mainly written for practitioners of educational evaluation - people who commission and perform educational evaluation and people who affect and are affected by it. For another category of audience (theorists, methodologists and empiricists), found mostly in the Western industrialized world, we can only say that there is a challenge ahead, namely that of facing the practitioners in their day-to-day "real world" before advocating any recipe for educational evaluation. To our last but equally important category of audience - evaluators, researchers and students - we hope that they will understand the difficulties encountered in the writing of this book.

Educational evaluation, particularly in the context of developing countries, is a challenging area of growth and should prove so for some time to come. For our part, we recognize that the problematic issues, strategic approaches and full realm of pragmatic considerations remain, none the less, largely untapped.

Guide to the readers

This book consists of three integrated and mutually dependent parts. It attempts to present a comprehensive approach to educational evaluation as shown in Figure 1. This approach provides a frame of reference for an understanding of the watertight relationships between: (a) problematic issues in educational evaluation in the three domains of theory, methodology and operationalization; (b) strategic approaches to evaluating the various areas of education (here we consider primary education, literacy, and technical/vocational education); and (c) pragmatic considerations derived from practical experiences (here we include the evaluations of primary education in Mauritius, literacy in Ethiopia and technical/vocational education in Kenya). As the figure indicates, it has not been possible fully to consider a comprehensive approach to educational evaluation, since there are many other educational areas in addition to many other worthy evaluation experiences not contained in this work.

In Part One, some major theoretical, methodological and operational issues in evaluation, and educational evaluation in particular, are presented and discussed. In the theoretical section (1.1) some definitions and interpretations of the concept "evaluation" are given and their relative importance for the evaluation of educational programmes and projects is explained. The evaluation of educational programmes and projects is presented as a continuous process or "built-in system evaluation". The planning of an educational evaluation programme or project implies a series of questions to be asked and a series of answers to be given. The major ones are presented in this section. Finally, Section 1.1 proposes a holistic approach to evaluation where there is an interplay among various frame factors and their components. The methodological section (1.2) considers the contemporary methodological debates surrounding the reliability, validity, choice and appropriateness of different designs, techniques, methods and data bases for educational evaluation. Several evaluation designs and techniques (surveys, experiments, simulations, observations, etc.) are briefly presented and discussed. They are also approached from the standpoint of information collection, processing and analysis. Section 1.3 focuses on some major operational issues in educational evaluation. Questions about the organizational setting for evaluation are examined. The importance of the linkage between information, communication and dissemination in enhancing good-quality evaluation is discussed. Emphasis is also laid on the utilization aspects to be considered in evaluation and the relationship between evaluators and evaluatees.

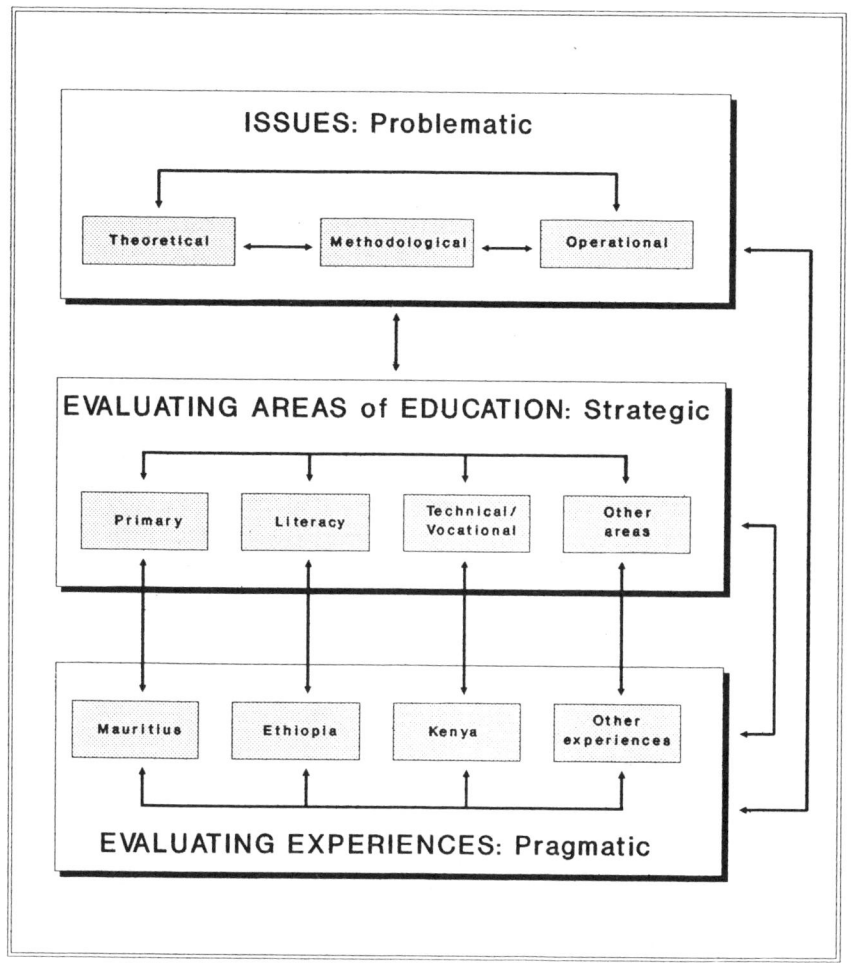

Fig. 1. A comprehensive approach to educational evaluation.

In Part Two, the real, practical world of educational evaluation is examined. It focuses on some important principles and practices in the evaluation of various educational areas: (a) primary education (Chapter 2); (b) literacy (Chapter 3); and (c) technical/vocational education (Chapter 4).

Chapter 2 begins with a presentation and examination of the aims and objectives of primary education in contemporary systems of education. This chapter treats some common evaluation designs (e.g. experimental, quasi-experimental, survey and naturalistic designs) with respect to the evaluation of primary school curriculum programmes. Then some major parameters for primary education evaluation (e.g. sampling procedures, evaluation instruments and data management) are presented and discussed.

In Chapter 3 the aims and objectives of literacy programmes are first and foremost critically examined. After considering the scope and coverage of literacy evaluations, the particular objectives of the evaluation are reviewed. The choice of appropriate designs for evaluating literacy programmes is also dealt with, together with a review of indicators and variables, and relevant sample lists. Finally, data-collection procedures and data analysis are discussed and commented upon.

After a presentation of the aims and objectives of technical/vocational education, Chapter 4 reflects upon the overview made of a number of evaluation studies within this field. Drawing upon this overview, the programme setting for the evaluation of technical/vocational programmes is then considered. Further, the various components which need to be taken into consideration are explained and discussed. Finally, evaluating overall programme performance is developed within the realm of technical/vocational education.

Part Three of this book deserves special consideration. To us it is the core of the entire work as it attempts to breach the gap between the rhetoric of educational evaluation and its practice. What is attempted is to focus on concrete practical experiences in educational evaluations. The three evaluations under consideration are all from developing countries. Much of the structure of Part Three draws upon the ideas presented, if not professed in Parts One and Two. Here, we are able to understand not only the lacunae in educational evaluation in these countries, but also the difficult conditions under which evaluation has to operate. All three experiences highlight the importance of capacity-building in educational evaluation in the developing countries.

There is little need to talk about the centre-periphery relationship in educational evaluation. Instead, the mutuality or interdependence between North and South in this field needs to be addressed. Much needs to be done and very little of what is done is conducive to the needs and expectations of countries in both North and South. It is true that some aspects of contemporary educational evaluation designs, methods and instruments are relevant to the evaluation of programmes and projects in developing countries, but in the course of their implementation, other more important issues are to be considered. These are treated in greater detail in the three remaining chapters, namely, "The National Educational Evaluation Study of Primary Education in Mauritius" (Chapter 5), "The Ethiopian Literacy Campaign Evaluation" (Chapter 6), and "The Evaluation Study of Industrial Education in Academic Secondary Schools in Kenya" (Chapter 7).

The final section, "Conclusions and Major Recommendations", serves as a forum for highlighting some of the major conclusions of the book. Recommendations are drawn up which largely address the issues of educational evaluation in the developing countries. Here, the particular evaluation and research climate in the developing countries is addressed and strategies for South-South co-operation as well as modalities for capacity-building in educational evaluation are presented.

This summary cannot do justice to the detailed presentation and discussion presented in the book. For the reader, it is of value to note that a brief summary is also included with the introductions to each of the three parts. As espoused in this book, there should be a holistic approach to educational evaluation; what this means for the readers is that much has been left unconsidered. The authors would be grateful for critical comments and reactions to this work. It is hoped that the arguments and issues here, and included in the holistic approach to educational evaluation, will be amplified and further developed by scholars in the field, particularly those from the developing countries.

Part One

Theoretical, methodological and operational issues

Introduction

Educational evaluation is an integral part of educational policy-making, planning and implementation. However, it is often regarded as an "end-of-product" exercise meant to assess the extent to which educational policies, plans, programmes or projects are successfully, effectively and opportunely implemented. Such a tendency persists even today in many educational evaluation activities. In Part One of this book, an attempt is made to reconsider the nature and characteristics of educational evaluations and their theoretical, methodological and operational implications. To start with, educational evaluation should be regarded as a continuous and permanent field of information processing built in to the life-cycle of an educational programme or project. As Dave (1979) argues, the "built-in process evaluation" draws upon the interactions and linkages among all the elements in a programme, namely its inputs, processes and outputs. In this regard, educational evaluation should neither be a fault-finding nor only a one-shot exercise.

Theoretically speaking, educational evaluation or the evaluation of any social intervention programmes is value-loaded. Educational programmes and projects cannot, in principle, be designed and implemented without going through consensus or coalition formation among different political, socio-economic, administrative and executive bodies. Evaluation can often be used as a tool to legitimize consensus among various interest groups while leaving out the possibility of managing conflicting issues and situations.

Much of the methodological debate about educational evaluation centres on the importance given to "technical rationality" in the selection of evaluation approaches, methods and techniques. The success of any educational programme or project depends upon a number of factors, some of which cannot be evaluated through traditional macro-economic or mathematical models. There has been a tendency to polarize evaluation approaches, methods and techniques into quantitative and qualitative ones. This polarization has greatly contributed to a narrow perception of the success or failure of given educational programmes in that evaluation became either "output-oriented" or "process-oriented". In fact, any successful educational evaluation should incorporate both intertwined dimensions. Genuine evaluation should adopt an open-ended strategy. It should benefit from the complementary roles that different methods and techniques can contribute to improving: (a) the quality of the information base; (b) the choice of evaluation instruments; and (c) the information processing, analysis and reporting.

Educational evaluation becomes more and more complex for programmes or projects that are by nature designed to involve multiple actors and serve multiple users. From the operational standpoint, the evaluation of such programmes or projects cannot be ensured without proper and effective co-ordination and communication linkages. Here again, an open-ended strategy is required in order to ensure the participation of various actors and beneficiaries in the different phases of the evaluation. The same goes for the choice and selection of appropriate evaluation methods, techniques and instruments.

1. Evaluation: an overview

The field of evaluation has seen much change and growth in the last thirty years. Much of this growth is due to the continuing efforts to promote progressive social change with successively more efficient, and more effective, programming. Berk and Rossi (1976) have pointed out that the impetus for much of the growth of evaluation activities is the "evaluation research lobby", which includes legislators, planners, programme managers and foundation executives. It is they who have been the driving force behind the growth and application of evaluation.

Evaluation researchers do not work within a social vacuum. It is important to remember that they work in a political context and are often either advocates or opponents of social action philosophies. Thus, they too are subject to bias. Policy-makers, as a whole, will prefer programmes that deal with social not psychological behaviour, and evaluations that deal with measures of performance not of capacity. The policy-makers will be more concerned with results that can show enduring changes, especially regarding community behaviour.

Evaluation is a vital component of almost any programme that wishes to remain competitive. Evaluation becomes the watchdog of efficiency in the planning and implementation phases, and the guarantor of effectiveness in the end results. More specifically, evaluation can be viewed as the systematic application of social research procedures in assessing the conceptualization, design, implementation and utility of a project or programme. As a process, evaluation can be seen as an attempt to assess the relevance, effectiveness and impact of an intervention, usually in light of its objectives.

The cost of an evaluation can be justified as it can in turn reduce substantially the overall costs of a programme. Evaluation, besides improving the planning and implementation of programmes, can lead to a better utilization of the available resources. In addition, evaluation results can influence decisions both in implementation and in the future planning of a programme. During implementation it may prove necessary to cut costs, to improve efficiency or to increase the magnitude of the programme in order to increase its impact. For future planning, evaluation results can influence decisions on the expansion, continuation or termination of a programme.

There are a number of factors which influence the use of evaluation information. These include the relevance and credibility of the evaluation as a whole, the way in which evaluation information is shared, the information processing of administrators and the degree to which potential users are involved in the evaluation. In considering the administrators' or policy-makers' self-perceived information needs, an evaluator can provide more relevant, timely and thus more useful evaluation information.

There is a need to pay greater attention to organizational problems, for it is often here that evaluation faces its many challenges, and it is here that evaluation's future opportunities are largely to be found. There is a need to examine the types of organization that are best for evaluation within varying social and cultural environments, and there is a need to develop and support evaluation units within these organizational settings.

1.1 The theoretical framework for evaluation

Conceptually as well as methodologically, the evaluation of an educational programme or project has often been limited to a given phase of a cyclical or chronological process. Educational evaluation is therefore commonly referred to as an exercise in assessing the success or failure of the planned objectives of a programme after it has been implemented but not before or during implementation (Chinapah and Fägerlind, 1986). This type of evaluation is often referred to as "product evaluation" or "outcome evaluation". In this section, the theoretical framework for evaluation is presented and discussed.

The nature and role of evaluation

Evaluation can be considered a process of analysis and control designed to determine the relevance, effectiveness, significance and impact of specific activities and the degree of efficiency with which they are carried out. At the same time, evaluation is more than the application of methods. It is a political activity and it is often now considered an essential part of managerial activities. In addition, it is part of a large stream of activities which lead to policy-making and effective planning and programming. Evaluation can determine a programme's impact and cost-effectiveness. A successful programme will reveal desired change or the achievement of stated goals. An evaluation of a programme's impact should be able to show whether or not the change or changes noted are a result of the intervention, and not the consequence of other factors external to the programme. The cost-effectiveness of a programme refers to its efficiency, or more specifically, its beneficial impact in relation to its costs.

Scarce resources underline the importance of cost-effectiveness and present a problem for programmes which are not efficient.

There is no doubt that evaluation can take on many roles, depending upon the context in which it is implemented. It could be an ongoing activity that parallels the development and implementation of a programme; it could be an ad hoc intervention; it could be a pilot project or programme assessment; or it could examine only the impact and effects of a programme: as in the case of an ex-post evaluation which is implemented once the programme is in operation or after its completion.

Accountability is one of many roles evaluation can fill. Accountability can cover a wide range of concerns, from matters pertaining to process and impact, to wider concerns such as a programme's fiscal or legal status of accountability. Continuous evaluations are often used to assess process accountability. On the other hand, cross-sectional evaluations can be employed to assess the impact and costs of a programme at particular points in time, which can be compared to the accrued benefits. In recent years, it has become more common, especially for larger programmes, to employ both continuous and cross-sectional evaluations.

Concurrently, one can argue that evaluation serves several purposes: perceived, unperceived, effective and at times conflicting. Familiarity with these various functions makes an evaluator better prepared to design, implement and adapt an evaluation as smoothly as possible. Evaluation can be utilized to improve or adapt an ongoing programme, or it can be used for accountability, certification or selection. The former is often referred to as a formative function, and the latter as the summative function. These two together largely account for the perceived functions of evaluation. Among its unperceived functions, evaluation serves a psychological or socio-political function which, while not obvious, can stimulate motivation or increase awareness. Further, evaluation can allow those with authority the ability to exhibit it. This is often referred to as the administrative function.

Evaluation is often also a political activity, as emphasized above. It plays a role in the decision-making process and affects the planning, design and implementation of projects and programmes. It also plays a role in deciding whether or not a programme will continue or be expanded. In this capacity, it rises above regular social science activities and becomes a political decision-making tool. Any body of information that assists in decision directives for programmes or interventions could be regarded as evaluation research. For some, mere impressionistic judgements are considered as within this realm. At what is perhaps the other extreme lies the belief that evaluation research is limited to purely empirical assessments of human resource programmes so that it is possible to determine whether or not they are useful. Evaluation can also be considered to encompass a whole progression of activities from conceiving and collecting data, to communicating and using data.

Rossi (1982) has identified three classes of evaluation research: (a) analysis related to the conceptualization and design of interventions; (b) monitoring of programme implementation; and (c) assessment of programme utility. Besides complementing monitoring, auditing and inspection, evaluation can attend to the creation of new knowledge and assess its effectiveness in application. It is also possible and preferable to think of evaluation as systematically being built in throughout the phases of the planning cycle (e.g. pre-planning, formulation, approval, execution, implementation and evaluation). This type of evaluation would focus on the continuous assessment of the programme concerned. The design, instruments, data and analytical techniques should, in this case, also reflect this holistic approach.

While evaluation can play a role in decision-making, in practice there are not many instances where decisions are made only on the basis of evaluation results. It is more often the case that evaluations simply influence the determinates of decisions which can take many forms. Evaluation results may simply contribute to the knowledge and experience of those that make the decisions without visibly affecting the immediate decisions at hand.

A further issue, of a more controversial nature, is whether a programme conducts its own evaluations or whether the evaluation is conducted by outsiders. In deciding which course to take, there are some specific arguments which must be weighed. In order to design and conduct an evaluation, one must know a great deal about the programme under examination, yet if a programme staff member conducts the evaluation, there is the risk that he or she may be biased, or that the results will not be considered valid outside the programme. The evaluation of established programmes are usually handled by programme staff. These evaluations are often a response to managerial concerns with maintaining or strengthening a programme's effectiveness and efficiency.

Types of evaluation

In recent decades there has been an increasing awareness of the need to systematize and defend the purposes and methods of educational evaluations. This, in turn, has led to a growing body of literature that challenges and defends the various evaluation models. Generally, there are three different types of evaluation which can be specified according to the areas to which they ascribe themselves. If an evaluation assesses whether or not a programme or intervention has been implemented correctly and according to its guidelines, it can be considered a process evaluation. On the other hand, there is the impact evaluation, which, as its name implies, is designed to assess the impact a programme or intervention has had on its intended target group and objectives. A holistic evaluation should include the activities of both the process and impact evaluations.

A process evaluation (often referred to as a "formative evaluation") is concerned with the manner in which a project or programme is implemented, especially as this regards the stated guidelines and design. It is further concerned with whether or not the programme is directed at the intended target group. A process evaluation should attempt to pinpoint the many problems or hindrances that can interfere with implementation. Some of these may include the situation where staff and equipment are not available, or where political forces prevent their allocation. Perhaps the programme staff are not motivated or are not properly prepared for their assigned duties, or perhaps it is the target group which presents difficulties, especially if they cannot be recruited or identified properly.

The programme staff often prove to be a hindrance. However, understanding and co-operation can be cultivated by the evaluator. Programme staff frequently perceive evaluation as extra work, or as a management tool for accountability. These perceptions can lead to resentment on the part of the staff. The evaluator should seek their co-operation and help them to understand the importance, and the opportunity for programme improvement, represented by evaluation. There are even some instances where explicit or written agreements are drawn up between the evaluators and the programme staff.

An evaluation study which is essentially only concerned with a programme's implementation and how to improve its effectiveness must observe the programme in operation, seeing its functioning at first hand. A post-programme assessment will not provide realistic recommendations in this area. A new area that should be considered by process evaluation is design or planning evaluation. This would in part, appraise the need or needs for a particular programme and the ability of the programme to satisfy them. There is still much work to be done with process evaluation, especially within its area of design. There also remains the need to develop uniform methods and theory for measuring implementation.

An impact evaluation (often referred to as an "outcome" or a "summative evaluation") is concerned with measuring the extent to which a programme produces the desired change. It does not necessarily need to assess the implementation of a programme. This type of assessment requires, of course, a set of operationalized objectives to be used as criteria for success. Impact evaluations have little meaning without relevant qualitative and especially quantitative data which can assess the extent of an intervention's effectiveness. Thus, experimental designs are often useful in impact evaluation because they can provide the most precise assessments.

Most impact evaluations do not consider the many factors external to the actual programme that can account for some or all of the noted unforeseen outcomes. Many of the impact evaluation designs have yet to consider how to distinguish these external influences from the actual programme. Ideally, an impact evaluation should be able to attribute change to the implementation, while ruling out other possible factors which might have affected the change. Further, an impact evaluation should be able to determine under what conditions a programme is most efficient.

A *holistic approach to evaluation* includes both a process and an impact evaluation. It is best for evaluations to include both types as they complement and support each other, yet due to restraints in budgets or the inadequacy of planning, this is not always possible. When measuring impact by itself, it is difficult for evaluators to pass judgement on the approved criteria if these were adjusted in implementation during fine tuning. Likewise, evaluators cannot judge a programme to be successful just because it was implemented according to its design. They should know whether or not the objectives were met, whether or not the programme had an impact and, if so, whether or not it was a positive impact.

Evaluation as a comprehensive process also means that evaluators, programme staff and administrators will be working together in a more conducive atmosphere, contrary to the situation where the evaluator comes in after the intervention to judge the work of others. This latter relationship can often be unfriendly and unproductive.

Monitoring

Monitoring is a process that should be undertaken during the development and management of programmes. The monitoring of implementation is especially important for programme designers who can make changes during the development phase of the programme to avoid problems that may arise later on. Monitoring data can reveal the variances between programme design and programme implementation. Programme managers should also use monitoring during the operation phase to provide feedback on the programme's ability to affect the target group within the programme's means. In monitoring the implementation of programmes, it is very important to distinguish between internal and external factors. Very often, some of the factors impeding the implementation of programmes have nothing to do with the quantity or quality of inputs but with societal frame factors (political, socio-cultural and economic).

To assure smooth implementation, effective monitoring is necessary to provide empirical feedback to project personnel. There are many reasons for monitoring, not least the public demand for accountability. Programmes are constantly affected by the environment in which they function. Programmes frequently fail to realize their objectives because qualified staff are either not available or not motivated. It could be that they do not understand the objectives, or are influenced by political and economic concerns. It could also be that the programme is not reaching the target group it was intended for. These are only a few of the areas where monitoring can enhance and improve programmes.

Chinapah and Fägerlind (1986) have argued that monitoring supplements and complements a built-in evaluation system, where the latter principally considers the totality of all phases of the planning cycle. Thus, the proper monitoring of programmes and projects cannot be pursued without feedback from the built-in evaluation system where the planning, design, approval, execution, implementation and evaluation phases are critically assessed.

The newest development within monitoring is the Management Information System (MIS), often used by large-scale programmes. The MIS can provide systematic and current data on a regular basis, thus giving programme managers and staff the quantitative data they need to assure smooth programming. Monitoring data can have a number of uses, depending on who the sponsor is and what stage of development the programme is at. However, monitoring usually addresses itself to a specific group, namely front-line implementors of a given programme or project, for corrective actions and reconsideration of the operational strategies.

Planning an evaluation

A critique of evaluation has often started from the standpoint that the questions about the professional identity of evaluators, the characteristics of the beneficiaries and the criteria of outcomes have not been properly asked and answered. In this context, it is of interest to look at the ten basic questions in planning evaluation proposed by Sim Wong Kooi (1975) in Figure 2.

Pre-evaluations can help to clear the way for further evaluation work. These evaluability assessments can also help to determine if the evaluation implementation is appropriate for the programme. It is important to seek the collaboration of programme staff, sponsors and relevant policy-makers in developing objectives and choosing evaluation tasks for the evaluability assessment. While evaluability assessments are preliminary appraisals which do not include formal research, they can prove well worth their time and effort. The interaction with staff helps to inform and prepare them for the evaluation. These assessments also allow the evaluator to test various scenarios and programme options. Resulting from an evaluability assessment is a plan, ideally worked out with others concerned, which includes a detailed design of the evaluation, and a list of programme components to be analysed. Further, this plan should outline the necessary participation of staff and resources and consider how the results will be utilized. For those whose interest in this topic goes beyond its brief mention here, Rossi (1982) has pointed out a series of successive steps for conducting an evaluability assessment.

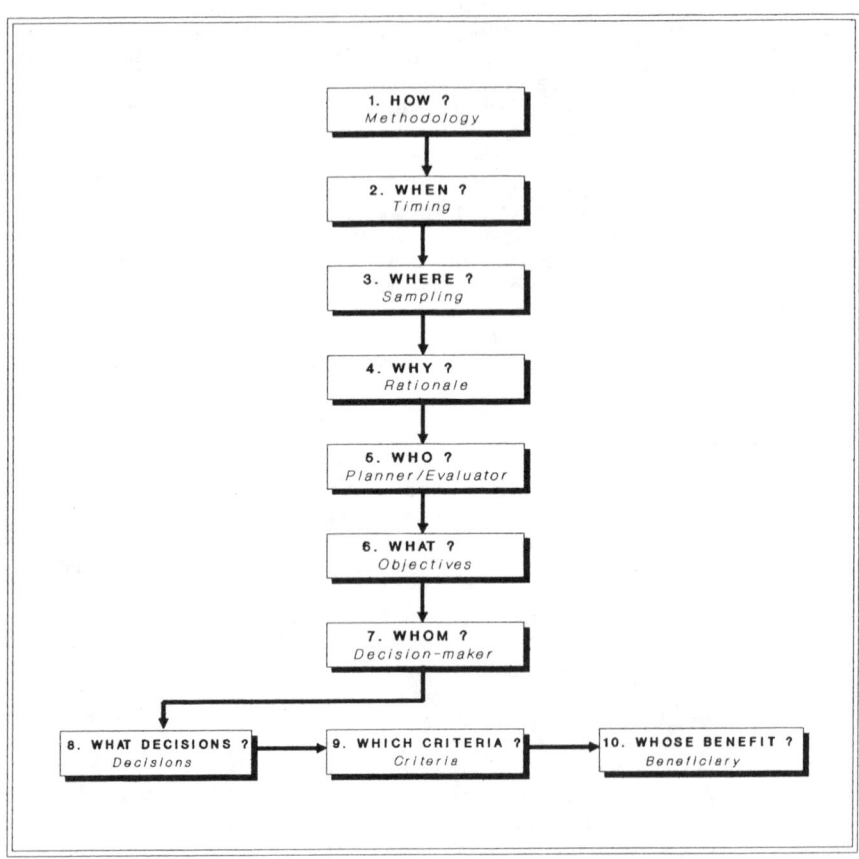

Fig. 2. Ten basic questions in planning evaluation. After Sim Wong Kooi (1975:190).

It should be noted that the role of the evaluator in relation to the evaluatees, and even in relation to the eventual information users, is changing. The ten questions proposed by Sim Wong Kooi (1975) and the relationships between them would in principle determine the type of programme one is evaluating and the different actors, users and beneficiaries involved. Participatory evaluation is sometimes suggested as a strategy to control for conflicting needs, interests and expectations in order to reach better results. How to accommodate for this strategy is an important methodological question. Generally, evaluators have an identity of their own.

They should be recruited outside the arena of planning, executing and implementation of the particular project or programme under assessment. They should be unbiased and as objective as possible. Their findings and recommendations should be brief and simple enough for quick and practical decisions to be made by their employers--the state, donor agencies and other institutions. Factual information is important while information of a qualitative nature (soft data) is not always given the role it deserves. In other words, whatever the tasks set for evaluation and the techniques and methods used, the danger of a stereotyped personality, procedures and information base is inevitable. If one follows the ten questions raised in Figure 2, such a tendency should not persist. Participatory evaluation would then be possible on the condition that these questions are properly answered in the development and application of appropriate techniques.

Evaluation, as mentioned above, is also commonly referred to as an exercise in assessing the success or failure of the planned objectives. In light of this, one may find it both entertaining and alarming to hear politicians, and at times programme planners and staff, talk of the successes of their programme when there are no set standards and data to justify or judge their assertions. To avoid this dilemma, evaluation of an educational programme or project should begin with a thorough analysis of the project or programme objectives. The evaluator should, further, look for the "implied" or "silent" objectives which do not appear in the documents and policy statements that spell out an educational project or programme. Comparison or reference should be made with both the immediate and the long-term objectives of the project or programme (see also Grabe, 1983).

In referring to objectives, we should emphasize the desired state to be reached or maintained through one or more activities. The objectives that the evaluator establishes can be divided into absolute and relative objectives. An absolute objective would require that an undesirable situation be eliminated or a desirable one be achieved for all. A relative objective requires the achievement of some set proportional improvement of conditions at some specified point or points in time. If the objectives are to be measured by outcomes that can be measured directly, then there is a much greater likelihood that the evaluation will be deemed competent. As we shall see later, this competency can affect an evaluation's relevancy, effectiveness and utility.

Objectives can further be divided into immediate and development objectives. The development objectives refer to broad sectorial objectives which the projects, with their more limited and immediate objectives, help to achieve. The project and programme evaluation concerns itself with differing sets of questions and criteria depending upon the immediate and development objectives for which it is designed. For example, a pilot project will concern itself with the question of generalization in the evaluation of a programme. Project-level staff, and those that design the project, often confuse objectives with means and methods and with planned outputs. It must be kept in mind that the immediate project objectives fit into the overall development objectives. If an evaluator notes any stray misconceptions at an early stage, corrective action can realign the immediate objectives with the development objectives. The United Nations Development Programme (UNDP) follows such an argument very closely in its new manual (February 1988) for the preparation and evaluation of programmes and projects.

Evaluating educational programmes and projects

Education, like any other social programme, is usually developed, in response to social problems. Thus, the programme becomes an organized effort to deal with the evident problem or problems. For example, the problem of unemployed youth resulting from urban shift in the Fiji Islands was combated with programmes designed to impart employability skills or to limit the demographic shift. Literacy campaigns usually result from the recognition that illiteracy poses a problem for the development of a country or group of people.

Education as such is closely associated with purposeful and organized social intervention programmes in the broader spectrum of human resource development. It conditions and is conditioned by a number of endogenous and exogenous forces, whether of a political, economic or socio-cultural nature. Fägerlind and Saha (1983) view the relationship between education and society as a dialectical one where education is part of a dialectical process with the economic, social and political dimensions of society. The dialectical process assumes that education: (a) is a product of society; (b) then acts on society by bringing about changes; and (c) acts again on the education system. As a consequence of these contradictions, the dialectical process may or may not involve struggle or conflict. The changes may be gradual or revolutionary ones. Thus, it is important to note that in evaluating educational projects and programmes, one must utilize data from the various dimensions of the social settings in addition to the required educational data. In order to capture: (a) the dialectical relationships between the societal factors (political, socio-cultural and economic); (b) the feedback linkages in planning, implementation and evaluation; and (c) the interplay among the three mutually inclusive components of an educational plan, programme or project (inputs, processes and outputs) to arrive at a systematic choice of appropriate techniques, good-quality educational evaluation should be based on a holistic approach. This approach is built upon an interplay among these three sets of frame factors conditioning the choice of appropriate techniques for educational evaluation as shown in Figure 3.

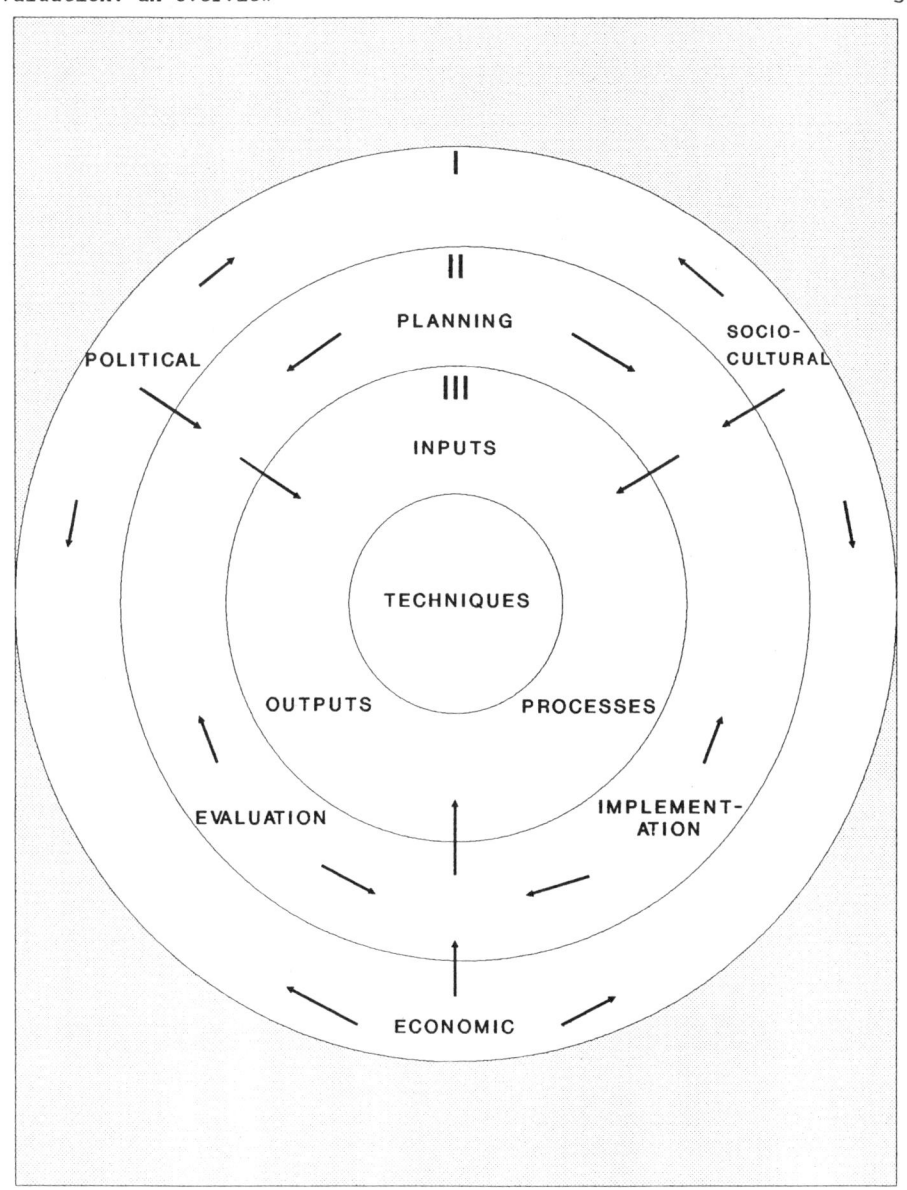

Fig. 3. Interplay among frame factors and their components. After Chinapah and Fägerlind (1986:46).

The holistic approach emphasizes the treatment of these projects and programmes in their unique and particular settings while at the same time understanding them in the form of their interdependence and interrelationships as wholes. Seen in this light, the evaluation of these programmes and projects requires a comprehensive design to examine their implementation, and the integration of different techniques to map the success of each.

The targeted clientele of educational programmes or other social action programmes are by nature very heterogeneous and their needs, interests and expectations are hardly unidimensional. Conflicting situations arise when educational priorities are set and resources deployed. Without a proper understanding of the human factor or the human purpose of educational projects and programmes where conflicts are inevitable, evaluation becomes more difficult and to a greater extent less useful.

Educational projects and programmes are much more specific than the larger dimensions of the educational policies they often make up. However, it is important to see them within the framework of global and specific educational policies. Chinapah and Fägerlind (1986) argue that it is practically impossible to evaluate educational policies without having systematically organized them. In this context, policy-analysis methods can be used. For evaluation purposes, educational policies are grouped in terms of operational educational programmes and projects and organized in accordance to their specific clientele system, for example, by level of education, by target groups or by geographical areas.

A project is normally understood to be a smaller unit than a programme, and can be considered as an element of a more comprehensive programme. A project can refer to an undertaking within a single management, designed to achieve specific objectives, within a given budget and amount of time. A programme, on the other hand, can refer to an organized set of activities, often with several management bodies, which is directed towards the attainment of specific but relatively longer-term objectives. Evaluation and monitoring may therefore have different emphases. However, it is imperative to consider the complementary processes of both. They usually converge on the same goal, namely that of improving the effectiveness of programmes and projects. Unesco (1982b:1-2) presented a strategy for the monitoring of literacy programmes in which the distinct and complementary features of evaluation and monitoring are discussed. These considerations are valid for the evaluation and monitoring of different educational programmes and projects.

The role of evaluation in improving the planning and implementation of projects and programmes is becoming more and more commonplace. Important questions will continue to be raised about the extent to which programmes operate efficiently and within their fiscal, legal and operational boundaries. Thus, evaluation will continue to preoccupy those involved with projects and programmes. For projects and programmes, increasing pressure is evident as the demand for efficiency assessments increases. In the coming years this area will probably be characterized by reduced resources and increased competition, just as it is today.

In this section, we have stressed that educational evaluation, just as the evaluation of any social intervention programme, requires a theoretical framework which incorporates, on the one hand, a built-in process evaluation design and, on the other hand, a participatory system including actors, implementation agents and beneficiaries. Without these features in mind, it is difficult to present and discuss any appropriate educational evaluation method or technique. It is also true that educational evaluation is a rather recent field of scientific inquiry. Therefore, there is a need for more theoretical and methodological developments in the field.

1.2 Methodological considerations

The theoretical development alone cannot meet the various challenges in the field of educational evaluation. It should be supported by appropriate evaluation techniques and methods. It is imperative to design appropriate methodological instruments which can capture the complex nature of programmes and projects in education. Development in methodology should not only be confined to techniques and methods for educational evaluation, as unfortunately, is often the case. It should also be tailored to the needs, interests and expectations of the entire clientele system (e.g. policy-makers, administrators and implementation agents of programmes and projects, funding agencies and beneficiaries of programmes and projects). An overview of such methodological considerations is presented in this section.

Many of the designs, techniques and methods used in evaluation were originally developed in other sciences and later adjusted to the field of evaluation. The technical-rational emphasis placed on them limits the possibilities of evaluating projects and programmes which are by nature highly sensitive and political (e.g. how to treat and measure the socio-cultural, political and human factors determining the success or failure of a programme's implementation). For this reason, many evaluation exercises have avoided the treatment and measurement of process indicators and have had recourse only to the input-output criteria that are mostly used for economic and business purposes. Some systematic reviews of evaluation techniques and methods with specific reference to educational evaluation are given in Gurugé (1971), Khan (1985) and Chinapah and Fägerlind (1986).

Perhaps it is the relative newness of the discipline of evaluation that has caused it to be dependent on other fields from which to borrow designs. Babbie (1973:52) argues that social science research and evaluation belong to the category of "easy sciences" and social scientists often require "a very sophisticated understanding of what conceptualization and measurement entail", an area which is thoroughly explored by the "hard sciences". This dependence is particularly clear when we consider the experimental designs adapted from psychology. These early adaptations focused on a programme's impact rather than on its development and implementation. They failed especially in not considering the social and political context in which a programme operates and which it is influenced by. Even today, the experimental designs utilized in evaluation prove quite effective in assessing the attainment of goals and objectives; however, they are not nearly as useful in assessing process. The model or strategy that is most suitable is the one which matches research methods appropriately to the evaluation questions being asked. Choosing the methods to be applied is often the most difficult step for the evaluator.

In the design of a methodological framework for evaluation, certain principles have to be observed. Some principles of evaluation focus only on the achievement of given educational objectives, i.e. to what extent the intended objectives of a given educational project or programme have been realized. Other principles focus on the causal effects and implications (total consequences) of a given project or programme *vis-à-vis* its targeted clientele - the beneficiaries. There are also some principles that lay great emphasis on a comparison of the causes and effects of two mutually related projects or programmes with the aim of judging which of the two has been more successful. The criteria of success may be their causes and effects on the targeted clientele, or the cost-benefit analysis, or a combination of both. In this context, the principles chosen for evaluation would determine whether an experimental, a quasi-experimental, a causal-modelling or a cross-sectional design is needed. A detailed examination of different principles of evaluation is provided by Alkin and Ellett (1985). For further reading on different types of evaluation design, see, for example, Babbie (1973), Patton (1980), Rutman (1984), Nachmias and Nachmias (1987), Wolf (1987) and Kidder and Judd (1987).

Choice of evaluation designs

An evaluation design should ideally consider the whole process of pre-planning, planning and implementation of an educational programme or project. Thus, it should be linked with the specific techniques applied in the collection, processing and analysis of data at the various phases of the programme or project. The choice of evaluation designs for the assessment of projects and programmes may vary as a result of the nature of the policies that are evaluated, or according to the type and quality of the information the evaluation intends to produce. Although longitudinal designs may be more appropriate for the particular evaluation at hand, it is often not feasible to apply them because the necessary resources are not available. Besides finances, these resources could include qualified personnel, computer hardware and software, a complete data base and a reliable communication-dissemination network. It is often these very basic prerequisites that are difficult to secure in developing countries. Under these circumstances, evaluation studies usually have to rely on other designs such as cross-sectional ones.

There are many areas within evaluation design that deserve attention and improvement, such as the present need to emphasize evaluation designs which yield results that are both credible and specific. In addition, the designers of evaluations have thus far paid little serious intellectual attention to the implementation of programmes. The choice of audience is also a justifiable design issue in evaluation studies, and as the importance of utilization grows, so too will the importance of the design issue.

There are several different study-designs available for evaluation purposes. A historical-descriptive study is a systematic description of a situation or area of interest that is factual and accurate. A case-study or field study is an intensive study of the background, current status and environmental interactions of a given social unit. This type of evaluation design has been noted for providing rapid information feedback. A true experimental study is an investigation of possible cause-and-effect relationships by exposing one or more experimental groups to one or more treatment conditions and comparing the results with one or more control groups not receiving the treatment (random assignment being essential). It should be noted that experimental designs are usually best applied in impact evaluations. A quasi-experimental study is a study which approximates the conditions of the true experiment in a setting which does not allow the control and/or manipulation of all relevant variables. This is a newer area, and evaluators are finding this approach more and more attractive and useful, especially when probing causal relationships. Evaluation design can be distinguished by noting the methodology to which it adheres.

Evaluation models

Educational evaluation covers a wide range of topics. While most educational evaluation models deal with teaching, learning and curriculum, some are designed to assess the practices and policies which facilitate them. Harnishfeger and Wiley's (1976) teaching-learning process model and Lundgren's (1977) model for the analysis of pedagogical processes are cases in point.

Evaluation models describe what evaluators do or at least order what they should do. Two types of generally recognized model are the prescriptive and the descriptive. A prescriptive model refers to a set of rules, prescriptions, prohibitions and guiding frameworks which specify what a good or proper evaluation is and how it should be carried out. A descriptive model is a set of statements and generalizations which describes, predicts or explains evaluation activities. Such a model is designed to offer an empirical theory. While prescriptive models provide the frameworks and strategies for carrying out evaluations, descriptive models provide a number of sound options for guiding the conduct of evaluation. The differences between prescriptive and descriptive models are great. However, with respect to this book, emphasis will be placed upon the prescriptive evaluation model, which deals more closely with specific programme evaluations.

A prescriptive evaluation model, when clearly understood and utilized, can prove to be one of the most useful tools available to an evaluator. It will determine which activities are appropriate, adequate, rational and just. It will specify the evaluator's obligations and responsibilities while giving advice, recommendations and warnings about how to carry out the evaluation. Three important aspects of a prescriptive model are its methodology, value and utility. These aspects can be used to classify evaluation models; however, it is likely that all of these aspects are either stated or implied in all evaluation models.

The valuational aspect of an evaluation model refers to its inherent desirability and worth, which could be measured by its usefulness or importance. It is also possible to distinguish between a model's extrinsic and intrinsic value. The extrinsic value refers to those properties which lend the model value as a means to something desirable, while the intrinsic value refers to the properties which are desirable or worthwhile as an end in themselves.

Evaluation models are guided by one or more principles; thus, familiarity with these basic principles assists in understanding evaluation models and the relationships between them. Alkin and Ellett (1985) provide a more thorough discussion of these principles in their article; however, a few comments may be helpful here. These principles provide insight into the purpose of evaluation activities and the methods required for achieving them. Many of these principles have limitations and have come under criticism. Some of them were developed to replace the previous ones which were deemed insufficient in accounting for the range of factors under consideration. A critical look at the order and development of these principles will also give an insight into the evolution of educational evaluation over the past few decades.

While some model-builders believe evaluations to be equivalent to experimental research methods, others feel that qualitative data provide the most important aspect of evaluation. For some, only the criterion-referenced testing procedures can produce suitable evaluations, while yet others focus their attention on causal-modelling, quasi-experimental procedures. A more recent group builds models with an emphasis on the concerns and interests of decision-makers and other users. Within this category of models the evaluator is often included as an adviser to the decision-makers, or as an educator for the users involved.

These various groupings of model-builders reflect the distinct differences in methodological approach. However, it should be noted that, as a whole, model-builders do not clarify their standing and commitment in regard to the particular methodological approach. It is also important to note that a large number of evaluation theorists feel that the causal efficacy of a programme should be examined in an evaluation.

Some evaluation techniques and methods

There is, quite obviously, no single technique or method that can serve all of the varying roles and types of evaluation. This becomes clear when we take account of the purpose and functions of a particular evaluation, as well as the varying information available for each particular evaluation. The techniques and methods available must be altered and adapted for each particular application. Perhaps the largest hurdle for the available techniques and methods is the leap across socio-cultural boundaries. Considering the further economic breach that separates the industrialized nations (where many of these techniques and methods are drawn up) from the developing ones, one can clearly see the care that must be taken in their application. This point underlines the need for further educational research initiated and developed in the Third World countries. Moreover, the methods will often have to be modified within each country in order to work effectively under the particular national or local conditions.

Evaluation must not always be limited to a single applied method. Two or more methods, when used properly together, can often prove to be complementary and more effective. When using methods in combination, it is perhaps better to apply one in a more stringent manner; this allows the evaluation study to be generalized. The other method or methods could be exploratory in nature and provide the study with supplementary information which could help in understanding the change that takes place as well as providing the evaluator with information that could guide further investigation.

The primary methods of evaluation involve surveys, case-studies or experiments, while the main techniques used involve sampling, interviews, questionnaires and observation. The specific methods and techniques chosen by an evaluator depend upon many factors, including the nature and disposition of the evaluation. The techniques used should take account of the evaluation results which are of interest to, and utilized by, the prospective audience. Understanding the way in which evaluation information is used is one way to improve techniques, or to apply them more effectively.

The recent history of evaluation has witnessed the development of better knowledge and technical procedures. The maturation of sample survey procedures, combined with more traditional experimental methods, has proved to be a very competent and effective means of assessing projects and programmes. Further developments in measurement, statistical theory, and the general pool of accessible social science knowledge and technical aids have allowed evaluation to make great advances as a discipline.

Two useful activities used by evaluators are formative studies and simulations. These are especially helpful assessments for innovative programmes which cannot build upon the experience of similar programmes. Formative studies are used in the design and development of a programme. They may include the assessment of a programme on a limited scale, or they may test a small sample of the intended target group. Not only do formative studies provide valuable feedback during the design stage; they also allow the opportunity to pre-test the evaluation procedures and instruments. Formative studies involve the evaluator in the planning process. While this may increase the successful planning and implementation of a programme, it also leaves the evaluator personally involved; the evaluator then becomes an advocate and participant in addition to his or her role as evaluator.

Programme simulations can either complement formative studies or, if time and costs limit their use, they can serve as guiding substitutes. Simulations can be highly quantitative (even using computer-based modelling) or they can be qualitative in approach and use: for example, scenarios to help predict the consequences of various alternative decisions.

Simulation technique is a powerful tool, built upon statistical and mathematical operations to calculate the consequences of postulating alternative values to parameters (exogenous and endogenous) to reach the optimal solution to a given problem area. Simulation technique consists of, on the one hand, a system and, on the other, a model. Wilcox (1985) has explained that the system may be almost any set of interrelated elements, while the model represents that system in the form of a corresponding descriptive or mathematical model. In the evaluation of educational programmes, parameters are often controlled or manipulated in order to reach a satisfactory solution. The parameters in a simulation model may be fixed, under control or invariant. For example, unit cost per student parameters may be kept controlled, allowing class size and survival rate parameters to remain invariant. The presence of a solid data base is important to make optimal use of the simulation technique. The simulation model can only be used with an organized information system.

The quality of the information needed and the quality of the results obtained from the application of simulation technique in evaluation is exceedingly different from the information needed and the results obtained from conventional techniques. Policy-makers are given a range of solutions for designing corrective measures to attain maximal internal efficiency of the project or programme. At the same time, they are offered the possibility of understanding how a small change in one or more measures could affect the input and output parameters.

Educational evaluation has inherited much of the tradition using complex mathematical and economic models. For example, many educational evaluation studies have used the so-called Educational Production Function (EPF) model in the assessment of home and school influences on students' achievement. The EPF model assumes that maximization of a given output can be reached through a combination of any given sets of inputs. "Schools are considered as firms, industries or production units designed to maximize the scholastic performance of children" (Chinapah, 1983a:118). Most educational evaluation and research studies of the 1960s and 1970s in both developed and developing countries were dominated by the EPF model (see Bowles, 1968; Levin, 1970; Simmons and Alexander, 1978; Schiefelbein and Simmons, 1979; Niles, 1981; Heyneman and Loxley, 1982; Chinapah, 1983a).

A number of evaluation techniques are unable to assess causality between the many input, process and output variables considered in an evaluation. However, the deterministic characteristic of survey technique ensures that the causal relationships between independent/predictor (input), intervening (process) and dependent (output) variables are simultaneously analysed. The survey technique usually ensures a wide range of quantitative data-collection methods through the application of structured questionnaires, interviews and checklists. Survey technique attempts as much as possible to satisfy the basic scientific characteristics for evaluation in the social sciences (Babbie, 1973).

One of the important functions of survey technique is to ensure that the evidence or empirical results are generalized from a sample or samples to a larger population. In evaluation, generalization is increasingly important as, for practical and economic reasons, data cannot always be collected on the entire population being surveyed. In surveys, the sampling designs (simple random sampling, probability proportionate to size sampling, stratified sampling, multi-cluster sampling, etc.) fulfil the prerequisite for generalization. In Chapter 2, sampling designs for educational evaluation will be discussed further. In the analytical phases, several statistical tests could be carried out to make inferences from the samples to the target population (chi-square tests, significance tests, etc.). It is the sampling techniques which can guarantee the representiveness and generalization of an evaluation study.

A condition for the conduct of evaluation is that it must be cost-efficient. This situation of resource-scarcity is prevalent in the educational programme budgets of most countries. Thus, survey techniques are exceptionally attractive as they create a condition where similar results can be obtained from a sample instead of from the entire population, thus saving time, personnel and financial resources. From the analytical perspective, educational surveys provide a large amount of data from various groups of informants. The strategy for analysis may vary from simple univariates to multivariates. The advantage of the analysis based on survey design is that various methods can be used to test a wide range of hypotheses through statistical procedures used in evaluation surveys. Some statistical packages like Statistical Package for the Social Sciences (SPSS) and Statistical Analysis System (SAS) are currently used for such purposes and include programmes for univariates (e.g. frequencies, means, standard deviations and condescriptive statistics), bivariates (e.g. cross-tabulations and simple correlations), and multivariates (e.g. multiple regressions, factor-analysis and path-analysis). In Chapter 5, an example of the use of survey technique for a national educational evaluation survey of primary education in Mauritius is presented and discussed.

As indicated earlier, qualitative aspects of projects and programmes can often be better evaluated through the application of various observation techniques or methods, such as: (a) participant observation; (b) case-studies; (c) documentary analysis; (d) content analysis; (e) field notes; (f) unstructured informal interviewing; and (g) checklists. Evidence from a wide range of evaluation and research studies focusing on quality in education has demonstrated that the designs, techniques, instruments and analyses often attribute great importance to quality input indicators that are quantifiable, measurable and crude. In-depth descriptive, open-ended, narrative types of information on determinants of success and failure of programmes are not considered properly in most phases of evaluation.

Observation technique belongs to the category of evaluation methods where a strong emphasis is given to qualitative evaluation designs, data-collection procedures, analyses and reporting. It is argued that observation data focus on the depth - instead of the breadth - of the information base and therefore provide detailed information for policy-makers, front-line implementors and programme actors as well as beneficiaries on what usually occurs in the implementation of the programme and how it works. Situations, events, interactions, behaviours, attitudes, beliefs, and so on, are summarized, systematized and simplified with no attempt at providing generalization or exact reproduction of them. Henceforth, in the application of observation technique it is necessary to consider the following limitations: (a) reliability and validity of the data; (b) generalization from the case-studies to the target population; (c) statistical inferences and hypothesis-testing; and (d) ethical issues encountered in the observers-observed relationship in the course of the evaluation.

Patton (1980) has drawn up five dimensions of variations in approaches to observation: (a) the role of the evaluator-observer; (b) portrayal of the evaluator roles to others; (c) portrayal of the purposes of the evaluation to others; (d) duration of the evaluation observations; and (e) focus of the observations. As for survey technique, participant observation technique can be used in a broader or in a narrower perspective depending upon resources available, time at disposal and needs of decision-makers and information users.

A variety of techniques have been used in the area of educational planning, administration and management. When the focus is on the implementation of large or extensive programmes, network analysis techniques (Gantt diagram, Programme Evaluation and Review Technique - PERT, and Critical Path Method - CPM) and management techniques (Management Information System - MIS) are among the most common evaluation techniques used. Some examples of these techniques as applied in the field of evaluation of educational projects and programmes can be found in *From Planning to Plan Implementation* (Unesco, 1982a) and *Pre-Service Training Programme in Educational Planning and Management* (Academy of Educational Planning and Management, 1984).

Policy-makers and planners are becoming increasingly concerned about the cost-benefit and cost-effectiveness of given educational programmes. Today, education commands a sizeable portion of the national resources of many countries. Thus, the growing concern for evaluation of resources allocated to the education sector may be viewed as a direct result of the competition for public resources from sectors of similar importance, such as health and nutrition. An enormous number of research and evaluation studies are carried out just for the purpose of investigating strategies for improving techniques for educational cost and finance and to look more closely at the implications of conventional budgeting techniques (for example, Planning-Programming-Budgeting System - PPBS).

The techniques presented and discussed can be optimally applied only if some basic requirements are satisfied first. These include a reliable information base, qualified teams of people using the technique and, if necessary, in-service training of the personnel involved.

Choice between quantitative and qualitative approaches

Educational evaluation requires the application of both quantitative and qualitative methods and techniques. The decision about which type of technique to use in the assessment will largely depend on the design of the evaluation as well as on the type and quality of information being sought. None the less, conscientious use of both qualitative and quantitative research together could result in more useful outcomes. As the discipline of educational evaluation develops further, there are likely to be advances in this area.

In recent years it could be said that more emphasis was being diverted from the traditional dominance of the quantitative approach, meaning the qualitative approach is increasingly being considered, especially in the literature of the discipline. Traditional qualitative methods include case-studies and participant observation. Traditional quantitative methods include randomized experiments and probability. Even today there still seems to be an unfailing debate between them. Questionnaires cannot duplicate or substitute for the field situation. However, qualitative notes from the staff in the field can complement the evaluation results.

There are several types of instrument used in quantitative evaluation designs. The most common are surveys with closed-ended questionnaires and interviews; cognitive and affective tests; and checklists. The limitation of these instruments is that the respondents are forced to express facts, opinions, attitudes and behaviours in a standardized format where the information is collected in accordance with predetermined response structures and analytical categories. Numerical values are then assigned to the responses from the items in the instruments and are analysed and presented in numerical format with tables, figures, matrices, and so on. It is only when instruments are tried on a small representative sample through pre-test design or pilot study that the evaluators and the evaluatees can interact among themselves in order to improve the quality of the instruments (format, presentation, clarity, reliability, scaling, etc.). Although many attempts have been made to include open-ended items in quantitative evaluation designs, still in the analytical stage, many of these data are treated in quantitative terms after they have been coded in some numerical form.

Table 1. Basic paradigms in educational evaluation

Dominant Paradigm	Alternative Paradigm
Quantitative	Qualitative
-concerned about reliability	-concerned about validity
-objective	-subjective
-distant from data	-close to data
-focused on impact of components	-holistic analysis
-concerned about outcomes	-concerned about process
-for scientists	-for practitioners
-large samples	-case-studies
-interested in generalizations	-interested in uniqueness
-tends to ignore interactions	-picks up individual treatment interactions

Source: adapted from Patton (1975:40).

In choosing an evaluation design, a decision must be made as to whether to focus on the depth of the educational issues under evaluation or on their breadth. In the latter case, one resorts to the application of quantitative designs that are mentioned above. The qualitative evaluation methods usually rely on detailed descriptions of people, events, situations, interactions, observable behaviours or direct quotations from people about their experiences, needs, attitudes, beliefs and thoughts. When contextual studies are used as qualitative methods of evaluation, excerpts from documents, correspondence and records are often used. Observation techniques - unstructured informal interview techniques, field notes, case-studies, specimen records and anecdotes - are among the most common qualitative evaluation techniques used. The general rule of thumb is to concentrate the evaluation exercise on a limited number of educational issues, involving few subjects, but collecting and analysing very detailed data on these issues and subjects. Patton (1975) has argued that the application of qualitative evaluation designs and methods in the social sciences can be viewed as an "alternative paradigm" to the conventional "dominant paradigm". His distinction between the dominant (quantitative) and the alternative (qualitative) paradigm is illustrated in Table 1. These two types of paradigm can complement and supplement each other, depending on the nature and type of programme under assessment.

Information base for evaluation

The information base and data for various evaluations may differ in scope, coverage and focus but they should be comprehensive enough to serve the information needs for all phases of the evaluation.

Generally, before the selection of data and indicators for an evaluation, baseline studies, state-of-the-art reviews, documentary analysis or other types of diagnostic studies are needed. However, it is often the case that this important preparatory stage is frequently not followed and in the application of evaluation techniques, new sets of data are collected and new indicators are developed. Thus, many of these techniques are not used effectively and it often happens that some kinds of data are abundant while other kinds of data that may be vital for proper planning and policy-making are scarce or incomplete. Relevance, quality, availability, reliability and validity are important characteristics for the development of the data base and indicators.

Survey technique has been considered an effective tool for evaluation. The data and indicators for survey may be cross-sectional or longitudinal. In the application of survey technique, the sampling design plays a significant role as data are not collected on the entire population. In this context, it is important to consider other data bases as feedback to survey data. The most conventional data base that can be used in these circumstances is provided by the periodic educational statistics usually available from the central statistical office in the respective countries. These statistics are usually presented quarterly, biannually and/or annually.

Survey data and indicators can be used to strengthen the data base by focusing on specific characteristics and needs of the target population. Survey data based on student files (e.g. personal characteristics, family background, home learning environment, educational expectations, attitudes towards schooling and peer-group characteristics), school files (e.g. school characteristics - type, region, size; as well as school facilities and services) and teacher files (e.g. teacher and personal characteristics - age, sex, qualifications, experience, socio-economic background; teacher attitudes and expectations; and methods of teaching) can also be used. Univariate, bivariate and multivariate statistical analyses can be carried out on the separate files as well as on the merged student, school and teacher files to provide descriptive and inferential statistics from the sampled data sets.

Conventional educational statistics together with survey data and indicators provide a solid information base. However, like many other evaluation techniques, the survey technique can only be used optimally when certain fundamental conditions are fulfilled (e.g. a reinforcing political and organizational climate for data collection and data reporting, qualified and skilled personnel and the availability of computer facilities).

To assess the quality or performance of a project or programme, observational data should prove most suitable. Observational data are of a more qualitative and descriptive nature. Patton (1980) has argued that such data are meant to describe: the setting that was under observation; the different activities that took place under that setting; the people who participated in those activities; and the meanings of the settings, the activities and their participation to those people. Implementation can then be approached in a twofold manner, i.e. from what has occurred to how it has occurred. Observational data can focus on various aspects of implementation: whether objectives set for the given programme have been attained as measured through classroom observation; teacher and student behaviours; interactions and activities among students in the classroom, and so on; whether the outcomes of the programmes differ according to the level of implementation across several classes or schools; the factors hindering or facilitating the implementation of the programmes; and the unintended or undesired outcomes observed in the course of their implementation.

Information obtained from observational techniques may be organized along three main dimensions: (a) data from rating scales; (b) data from systematic observation; and (c) data from unstructured observation (Lewy, 1977). Data from rating scales are usually subjective and should generally avoid quantification. Such data may refer to teacher and student attributes observed during the implementation of a given educational programme. Data from systematic observation are more structured and are related to fixed and predetermined events in the course of implementation. Quality-control measures are used here to check whether the expected outcomes are met in the implementation of the programmes. The outcome data are known, the topics or areas on which the evaluation should focus are identified and the observation schemes for recording events, behaviours, interactions, and so on, are prepared in advance. Unstructured observation is used to give a more informal and qualitative picture of how an event is implemented in the form of anecdotal records. Contrary to systematic observation, the data here tend to be less organized but allow the observer to record unexpected and/or undesired outcomes in the implementation of a programme. The analysis of anecdotal records is time-consuming and painstaking. However, much of the information that can be gathered through unstructured observation cannot be gathered effectively from rating scales or systematic observation.

During the course of the implementation of an educational programme, both quantitative and qualitative types of data are required on: (a) the organization/administrative linkages or barriers; (b) human and financial resource capacity and/or constraints; (c) the availability of administrative and managerial skills at the different levels; and (d) the system of evaluation or monitoring of the progress of the programme (record-keeping, inspection, supervision and reporting).

In his review of indicators of an educational system, Johnstone (1981:27) differentiates between three categories of educational indicators: (a) input indicators; (b) process indicators; and (c) output indicators. His definition of these three of categories of educational indicators is as follows:

Educational *input indicators* are either indicators relating the amount of a particular quantity taken by an education system to the total amount available for distribution, or indicators describing the aspirations held by a society for education systems.

Educational *process indicators* are those indicators describing the structure of the system which processes the inputs to become the outputs, or those indicators describing the distribution of the inputs throughout the education system.

Educational *output indicators* are either indicators relating the amount of particular quantity leaving an education system to the amount with some similar characteristic which is available to leave, or indicators describing the perception by a society of the results of the functioning of education systems.

Some of the more systematized techniques used for management and budgetary purposes have their own specific data needs which differ from the conventional data and indicators required for these types of assessment. For example, PERT (Programme Evaluation and Review Technique), one of the management techniques available, focuses on the implementation of a programme from the point of view of resources expressed in time and/or cost units of various activities. Henceforth, additional information is needed on the setting under which a programme operates. The selection of data and indicators for PERT is strictly related to the three steps that must be followed in the preparation of a PERT network, namely: the setting of events and activities; the data loading on the network; and the time-scheduling. Another such technique used in cost and finance evaluations, the PPBS (Planning-Programming-Budgeting System) technique, requires a systematic system of information and evaluation in order to provide rational budgetary choices for the use of resources in the attainment of the objectives of a programme. Since the emphasis on rational budgetary choices and alternative means to maximize outputs, this requires the selection of data and indicators that are visible and self-explanatory as far as the outputs are concerned. The PPBS technique requires input data (human, material and financial resources) and output criterion-indicators in order to compare the costs and advantages of alternative budgetary choices.

The PPBS technique calls for a comprehensive system information with a well-timed and accurate data base in order to review objectives of programmes and their continuous analysis. As the budget has to be self-explanatory, the information presented in textual and tabular formats must be simple and clear enough for the different users (e.g. legislators, planners, administrators and the general public).

In this section, we have focused on some major methodological considerations in educational evaluation. They cannot be properly understood without a direct "liaison" to the operational processes required in educational evaluation. In the next section, some common operational issues are examined with respect to the organizational setting for evaluation, utilization-focused evaluation and the relationship between evaluators and evaluatees.

1.3 Operational issues

The rising costs of programmes and the ever-decreasing resources available bring even established programmes into question. Evaluators cannot hope to increase their influence in decision-making by adapting the organizational setting to their ends, which may or may not result in better programming. They can, however, attempt to understand the organizational setting better, and in light of their increased understanding, improve and adapt their methods and techniques. Thus, evaluators should try to gain a better understanding of how the organizational setting influences the realm of evaluation, how it appraises evaluation results and how it utilizes evaluation, keeping in mind the many functions it can serve for them.

Organizational setting for evaluation

There are various difficulties that evaluations and evaluators must deal with in the course of their work. Problems in evaluation implementation occasionally arise as a result of resistance, or the lack of willingness to co-operate on the part of managers and other "stakeholders". This friction may occur because the stakeholders cannot grasp the purpose of the evaluation or because of outside pressure. It is often argued that the problems of implementation are not from the technical-rational arena, but are rooted in the socio-economic and political arenas. Yet another difficulty with the evaluations of projects and programmes is that the evaluation results are simply not used to improve and adapt the programmes they were intended for.

One of the major difficulties in the implementation of programmes and projects is the treatment of conflicting goals and conflicting interest groups. In both situations, the evaluation exercises become more demanding but fruitful. As

Chinapah and Fägerlind (1986) have argued, the management or institutionalization of conflict becomes vital for successful evaluation. This is only possible when participatory evaluation is ensured and where programme planners, implementation agents and the actual beneficiaries are involved. Good-quality evaluation can only be guaranteed through an information- dissemination system where there are both top-bottom and bottom-top flows of information and interactions along the horizontal as well as the vertical levels of educational planning, administration and management. It requires a political climate where self-criticism, inter and intra-administrative and departmental disagreement are tolerated.

The tendency to bring programme users closer to programme planning, implementation and evaluation has led to demands for a so-called "information-coordination-communication linkage". There is today an increasing interest in the users of evaluation information, i.e. from decision-makers through funding agents to target beneficiaries. This relationship between evaluators and users is increasingly being considered in models and strategies, and in turn it is changing the evaluation environment.

There are three general areas where progress can be made within this linkage. The targeting of interests and information needs of the users is perhaps the most important. Another is the careful dissemination of evaluation information and results with follow-up, and effective and relevant presentations with clear report language and appropriate depth for the users. These can improve the efficiency and utility of the evaluation process.

Utilization-focused evaluation

Evaluation results have many uses. They can influence the decision-making process, they can indicate accountability and validate programmes and they can add to the pool of social science knowledge. However, it should never be assumed that providing information will assure its use. Evaluation should have utilization as a driving force and the concern for an evaluation's use should be continuous and should be considered right from the initial planning stages. Utilization should be built into every step of the evaluation and should not be left to chance. To consider an evaluation's utility at the end of an evaluation can force one into adaptations and adjustments which can compromise the evaluation's intent.

An evaluation should be user-oriented and planned to provide useful information for the intended audience. Thus, one of the first things to do is to identify this audience of decision-makers and potential users and, ideally, involve them at every stage of the evaluation. This involvement will ensure that the evaluation addresses relevant questions and provides useful information. The scope of such a participatory evaluation can easily become too wide as the interests of the many participants are represented; thus, the content of the evaluation must be identified and focused accordingly.

The very nature of such a participatory approach should yield recognizable results that are of higher quality and are more extensively utilized. This approach should also be valued as a learning experience for all those involved, as their understanding and appreciation of evaluation are increased. The costs of such an evaluation will tend to be noticeably higher than for an evaluation which does not take such an extensive note of utilization; however, the benefits should easily outweigh these additional costs. The evaluator should make these costs evident in the evaluation proposal and budget.

The success of utilization-focused evaluations depends largely on the abilities of the evaluator, who must determine the potential users, facilitate their involvement throughout the evaluation, maintain sensitivity and respect for the varied interests and train the stakeholders in evaluation methods and processes, as well as help the decision-makers involved become more aware of the evaluation's use in planning. In orchestrating all this, the evaluator must be familiar with, and willing to apply, the appropriate techniques where such a linkage in information, co-ordination and communication is firmly established (see also Patton, 1978; Tyler, 1989).

After completing their work, evaluators often find that decision-makers do not share their enthusiasm and react slowly to the findings. This can be a disconcerting experience; however, evaluators must be prepared to adapt many personal and general features of their work in responding to such situations. The evaluator will also need to be more aware of various factors (community variables, organizational characteristics, the nature of the evaluation, evaluator credibility, political considerations and resource constraints) which affect the process and utilization of evaluation. At times the personal credibility of the evaluator may be more important that the quality of the methodology, a fact which is often overlooked by the information users. However, this may not be the case in highly controversial or politicized evaluations. It is important to note, perhaps, that utilization is not necessarily the most important concern to all evaluators, especially if they are working under different frameworks. None the less, it is important to consider threats to utility, just as we consider threats to validity. Both can seriously undermine the actual impact of an evaluation.

The stakeholders, including the sponsors, management and staff, and even at times the participants themselves, may try to influence the decision-making process. In some educational programmes (especially where students are afforded extra benefits of time, facilities or stipends for their participation), students and their parents involve themselves by pressuring decision-makers to continue the programme, even when local assessments find that the programme is not reaching the target group and national assessments find that it is not fiscally feasible.

Variables that affect the utility of evaluation include its relevance, communication between evaluator and user, the manner of information processing employed by the users, the credibility of the evaluation and the level of involvement of the potential user. Thus, to increase an evaluation's utility and relevance, an evaluator should try to understand the cognitive mode of action of the decision-makers, and pay attention to the timeliness of their work in regard to the user's needs. Further, the utilization and dissemination plans should be included in the evaluation design, and these should be assessed just as the other aspects of the design will be assessed within the wider context of the evaluation. If utilization is to be considered, as it should be, then the above considerations will prove helpful.

Perhaps the most obvious impact of an evaluation results from the new information it provides. Such information is spelled out in findings and recommendations, and can influence activities and attitudes. The impact of an evaluation can be intended or may be unintended. While evaluation information can have a remarkable impact on a programme or policy, it is usually only one of many sources that a decision-maker considers. Measuring the impact of evaluation information is difficult because it is one of many contributing influences upon decision-making. Problems can often arise with the diffusion of evaluation information. Yet perhaps the biggest complication is that the impact felt from the evaluation results is largely unobservable. In order to have a better understanding of the impact of evaluation information, it is important to consider the many unnoticeable influences it can have. None the less, evaluation information does have an influence and impact, and while the extent to which it is considered cannot be easily determined it is one of the contributing factors.

Evaluation information is frequently overruled by other considerations, yet the information may nevertheless have influenced individual decision-makers, and just being discussed and available for future input lends some merit even if it has no noticeable impact on the programme in question. Another hidden impact deals with the corrective feedback it provides. In such a role, its impact would only be conspicuous if a programme went astray. Otherwise the feedback would just assure those involved that things were in order. Even when a programme or policy remains unchanged by favourable feedback, an impact can be levied in the attitudes and beliefs of those with whom the information comes into contact. It can strengthen the thoughts of some while undermining the beliefs of others. Further, evaluation information can have impacts that are not necessarily planned or expected. It can bring together groups in the discussion, and it can divide people as it draws out divisions. Thus, the impact of evaluation information, while not affecting immediate actions, can have an impact as it affects attitudes and beliefs.

It is important to note that evaluations may in the end serve either the programme's supporters or its opponents. Information on how well interventions were implemented, the extent to which they met their objectives, their costs and their impacts is vital to all those directly or indirectly concerned with the programme.

The information can either serve to legitimize the programme or provide the rationale for discontinuing it.

Evaluators and evaluatees: how do they relate?

There is an extensive debate today on the professional identity of educational evaluators. The tendency has been to isolate the evaluatees in the debate and focus on the multiple roles an evaluator plays in the evaluation process for a wide range of clientele. Nevo (1985) has argued that the role of the evaluator depends largely on the way evaluation is perceived. Henceforth, evaluators may be controllers or auditors when their function is that of assessing the extent to which educational objectives are actually being realized. They are intelligence officers, public scientists or educators when their task is to provide information to decision-makers and the audiences for a better understanding of important educational issues. Finally, evaluators act as judge, referee or art critic where their judgement of the merit or worth of a programme is called for.

Insisting upon a watertight working relationship between evaluators and evaluatees is a challenge *per se*. Even at the conceptual level, room is rarely given to such a relationship. In his review of major actors in an evaluation process, Weiss (1984) could identify only three major groups: (a) evaluators; (b) decision-makers; and (c) evaluation funders. In this triangular process, the institutional settings of the three groups of actors play a decisive role and encompass reward, interaction and career patterns. Likewise, the state of the science and the state of the society serve as determinant elements in the evaluation process. Figure 4 shows the influences on key actors in the evaluation-decision system. Weiss (1984:166) argues that "each set of actors may be playing in the same game, but they are likely to be playing by a different set of rules". For example, the obstacles to programme planning, implementation and evaluation may be of both the intellectual/cognitive and the social/structural dimensions.

Some principles governing educational evaluation emphasize the active participation of the targeted audiences or prospective users of an educational programme in all phases of evaluation. However, much of this kind of participation is referred to as "token participation". Genuine participation in an evaluation requires, among other things, an effective information exchange between the evaluators and the evaluatees. The extent to which participant evaluation may be realized also depends on the political and bureaucratic climate under which an evaluation takes place. When an evaluation is expected to bring organizational changes or too much room for conflicting interests and needs, the rapport between evaluators and evaluatees may remain a distant one. In this case, both the evaluators and the evaluatees may be seen as potential threats to the political and bureaucratic audiences.

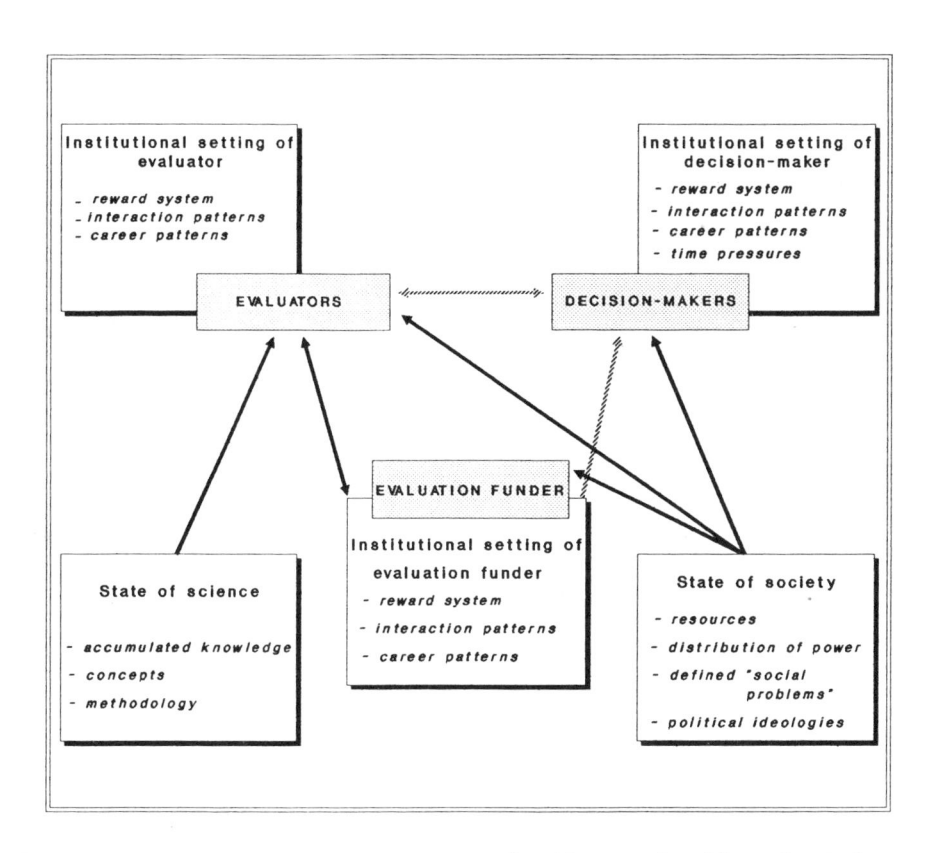

Fig. 4. Influences on key actors in the evaluation-decision system. After Weiss (1984:165).

Several educational evaluation programmes and projects have included the target beneficiaries in their design. For example, in school survey evaluation design and in classroom observation design, a certain progress has been achieved in this direction. In our case-study examples in Part Three of this book, some modalities for participatory evaluation in selected educational programmes will be presented and discussed.

When treating operational issues in educational evaluation, it becomes imperative for the evaluator to consider the actors, goals and outcomes of an evaluation, working closely with the actors to modify or transform the goals and objectives so that they conform to the expected outcomes. The involvement of the stakeholders at all stages of the evaluation process ensures their interests and that the evaluation matches their personal concerns and increases the evaluation's utility. Altering of goals may also result in changes in actors and outcomes.

To be most effective educational evaluation should be envisioned as a lengthy undertaking that must be developed and planned as the development and planning proceed on the project or programme it is to assess. However, there are times when, for various reasons, evaluation is undertaken after the project or programme has been implemented. For ad hoc or ex-post evaluations, it is difficult to retrace the development and planning of the programme or project. It is difficult to identify the immediate programme goals and development objectives unless they were analysed before implementation. It is recommended that the evaluation, whether planned in advance or developed as an ad hoc or ex-post evaluation, always begin with a thorough analysis of the objective. Thus, one of the biggest hurdles for ad hoc educational evaluation is precisely these narrow, short-sighted and simplistic attributes with which given educational programmes and projects are associated.

Without a proper understanding of the theoretical, methodological and operational issues in evaluation, and educational evaluation in particular, it may be difficult to elaborate in detail the nature, importance and implications of evaluating educational programmes and projects. One major purpose of Part One was to serve as a platform to examine the developments and debate in the field of evaluation of relevance to educational programmes and projects. In Part Two, we shall focus on some strategic approaches to evaluation in the area of primary education, literacy and technical/vocational education.

Part Two

*Evaluating specific areas
of education*

Introduction

There is a general consensus today that evaluation plays a more important role in the planning and implementation of educational programmes and projects than it did some years ago. However, much has yet to be achieved in this field, not least from the theoretical, methodological and operational standpoints as evident from the discussion in the foregoing chapters. There is also a strong conviction that it is neither possible nor appropriate to arrive at any "prefabricated menu" for educational evaluation as educational programmes and projects are multi-purpose and multi-dimensional in character. Like any other social intervention programme, they serve heterogeneous societal groups with often diverse interests, needs and expectations. In other words, there is a call for greater understanding of the nature and coverage of educational evaluation with respect to its contributions and limitations.

The decision to confine oneself to specific educational areas in evaluating educational programmes and projects is a step in the direction emphasized above. Part Two of this book focuses on some important principles and practices in the evaluation of programmes and projects in given educational areas. Three educational areas are chosen: primary education, literacy and technical/vocational education. It is important to note that the areas chosen and the designs and techniques proposed are by no means representative and care should therefore be exercised in using these examples for all types of educational evaluation programmes or projects.

Chinapah and Fägerlind (1986:13) argue that in the evaluation of an educational programme or project, the following aspects are to be considered: (a) organizational and administrative setting of the programme or project; (b) budgetary allocation and ceilings; (c) programme coverage (the target clientele); (d) logistics (availability of physical, material and human resources); (e) information-dissemination system; and (f) desired outputs.

In addition, the authors present a guideline for preparing and reporting an educational evaluation. The guideline consists of the following: (a) introduction and summary; (b) general objectives of programme or project; (c) selected programme or project objectives; (d) structure of the evaluation activity and report; (e) scope and limitations; (f) literature review--theory, concepts, methods and empirical evidence; (g) theoretical or conceptual framework for the evaluation; (h) methodology--sampling and target population, instruments and data-collection techniques; and (i) findings and recommendations.

2. The evaluation of primary education programmes

2.1 Analysis of aims and objectives of primary education

Educational aims and objectives are broad in nature and complex in character. They are generally a product of consensus and coalition formation among various interest groups in the planning and decision-making apparatus. However, for other groups like implementation agents (educational administrators and officers, school head-teachers and teachers) and target beneficiaries (the community, pupils and their parents), the broadness and complexity of aims and objectives are often reflected in ambitious and/or poor-quality educational plans, policies, programmes and projects. There is also a belief among those who have the mandate to perform some evaluation activities (for example, programme and project evaluators, school inspectors and teachers) that the general nature of educational aims and objectives contributes to poor-quality educational evaluation to the extent that basic questions such as: evaluation of what? for whom? why? by what means? and to what ends? remain unanswered or are kept hidden.

The analysis of educational aims and objectives is *per se* an important element of educational evaluation. Some progress has been made in this field. For example, this progress is marked by an improvement of guidelines prepared by some funding agencies in the design, preparation and evaluation of their educational programmes and projects. As mentioned earlier, UNDP's programmes and projects are structured along a hierarchy of objectives which leads to specific activities and outputs that both the agency and the recipient bodies can easily monitor and evaluate. Chinapah and Fägerlind (1986) argue that policy-analysis methods are important ingredients of good-quality educational evaluation and monitoring in that they serve as tools for evaluators and monitors to differentiate between programmes of a national development character, those specific to the education sector, those specific to given levels or types of education and those specific to a given educational project. Such a strategy permits evaluators and monitors to have a greater focus on their tasks, time and resources and henceforth helps them in the development and choice of relevant evaluation design, instruments, indicators and methodology.

It is important to stress at an early stage that there is more diversity than universality in the aims and objectives of primary education in the world's system of education. The first area of concern is the term primary education itself. In most countries, it means the first cycle of education. This first cycle is variously labelled elementary education, basic education or comprehensive education. Second, the length of primary education differs between countries and this difference is more pronounced between developed and developing countries' systems of education. The great majority of countries have a six-year primary education cycle, but among the remaining ones it may range between three and ten years of education. Third, in general the curriculum of primary education is dominated by language teaching and mathematics or arithmetic. Other subjects such as science, physical education, foreign languages, politics, religious or civic education and practical work are also taught. Fourth, with few exceptions, most of the teaching at primary education level is based on conventional teaching methods in the form of homework and classwork, question and answer and rote learning. Only in a few countries group learning, exploratory and experimental methods are used. Finally, some countries have chosen to allow children to move from one grade to the next through the system of automatic promotion. There is, however, a variety of ways in which pupils' skills and competencies are assessed and examined at this level of education, for example, through periodic teacher reports, intermediate cognitive tests and final examination tests. The most common examination takes place at the end of the primary cycle for selection and qualification to further studies or employment. Following pupils' progress along the primary education cycle is a matter left to the school and the teacher in a number of countries.

The foregoing analysis enables us to understand that the evaluation of primary education programmes should be tailored to the specific features of that level of education, bearing in mind a country's situational contexts. In the absence of any universal rule, it is therefore important to consider country-specific programmes for primary education in any evaluation exercise. Equally important is the fact that primary education, like any level or type of education, is exposed to forces both internal and external to the system. In this context, evaluation should be a continuous process to take account of the gap between the development of education, on the one hand, and the realities of life and realistic expectations, on the other.

The aims and objectives of primary education can be regarded as implicit and explicit expressed concerns of children, parents and teachers, and as hopes of the political and social leadership. One way of mapping these concerns and hopes is to review the overriding aims and objectives of primary education around the world. In Volume 38 of the *International Yearbook of Education* entitled *Primary Education on the Threshold of the Twenty-First Century* (Unesco-IBE, 1986), a comprehensive and systematic analysis of the aims and objectives of primary education in the world systems of education is presented. The analysis is based on the objectives assigned to primary education by eighty-four educational systems. The following three aspects of primary education are most frequently singled out as a priority objective, or sometimes the sole objective, of primary education. According to Unesco-IBE (1986:128-9) they are:

Basic knowledge and skills (these include both references of a general nature and specific references to reading, writing, arithmetic, etc.); the most questionable cases would be those where this aspect is singled out as the primary one among several others, with the obvious intention that these others should also be taken into account.

Overall education or development (of the pupil, the individual, the person, the personality, etc.); also included here are the objectives which specify in turn the various aspects - intellectual, moral, aesthetic, etc. - of this complete education.

A foundation for subsequent education (including some expressions of a distinctly individual type and even a few - somewhat reluctantly - which view primary education as a preparation for the secondary level).

Educational aims and objectives usually mirror the historical, political, socio-cultural and economic forces of a society and the routes that society has chosen for the future. El-Ghannan's (1980:62) synthesis of educational objectives in the Arab states is a case in point. He observes that educationists first divide qualities and abilities to be produced by the education system, namely, "knowledge which consists of the ability to absorb and remember information as part of intellectual development; the affective aspect which includes development in aptitudes, abilities and values; and the physical aspect which includes muscular abilities and physical development". The question remains which qualities and abilities are oriented to individual development and which to societal development. Similarly, educational objectives may be classified with regards to individual, social, economic, scientific, ideological, religious, civic, national and universal aspects but not all of them are always subject to educational evaluation.

In his discussion of the universal and the particular in educational goals, Boudhiba (1980:120-1) argues that most experts usually stress that the meaning of man is the final aim of education. Henceforth, "the African idea of self-sufficiency, the Arab concern with being master in oneself - with raising oneself to the level of one's own past and forging one's own destiny - the Latin American liberation ideal, the socialist dream of a new man and the integrity ardently demanded by the Asiatic are only variations on the same theme". In addition, educational aims and objectives differ first of all as to their degree of development. As mentioned above, most countries make the necessary efforts to provide children with basic skills and knowledge, to ensure their overall education and development and to lay a foundation for subsequent education. However, the extent to which these aims and objectives are successfully realized is a principal concern of an educational evaluation or evaluations tailored to country-specific primary education programmes and projects. This brings us to some examples of country-specific aims and objectives of primary education taken from Volume 38 of the *International Yearbook of Education* (Unesco-IBE, 1986:114-30).

Six country-specific aims and objectives for primary education are presented here, namely, those of the United Republic of Tanzania; the People's Republic of China; Brazil; the Syrian Arab Republic; England and Wales; and Czechoslovakia. Analysis of these aims and objectives reveals some of the general tendencies and country-specific characteristics of primary education. In other words, the universal and the particular goals of primary education as outlined by Boudhiba (1980) above deserve much greater attention when programmes and projects are evaluated. The aims and objectives of primary education in the United Republic of Tanzania are to: *foster the social goals of living together and working together for the common good; to give pupils a permanent ability in literacy; to impart the socialist values, attitudes and knowledge which will enable the pupils to play a dynamic and constructive part in the development of their society; to help the pupils develop an inquiring mind and ability to think and solve problems independently and to provide pupils with an education which is complete in itself, inculcating a sense of commitment to the total community and to help the pupils to accept the values appropriate to Tanzania's future.*

In the People's Republic of China, *the task of primary education is to educate children to be strong in morality, intelligence and physical constitution so as to lay a sound foundation for their secondary education. The targets are to educate them to love our socialism; to teach them how to read, write and calculate; to pass on to them some basic knowledge of nature and society; to cultivate their good habits of study, so that the students get properly developed both physically and morally, with strong physique and good habits of living and working.*

The general objective of primary education (first grade education) in Brazil is *to provide the pupil with the necessary training for developing his potentialities as an element of self-realization to qualify him for work and the conscientious exercise of citizenship.*

The Syrian Arab Republic lays great emphasis on the integrated aspect of primary education: *Primary education is aimed at the child's well-balanced and overall development in the physical, psychological, social, moral, national and emotional aspects, by providing him with certain notions and tendencies so that he can make his way in practical life as a citizen, worker and producer and continue his studies in the subsequent cycles.*

In England and Wales *primary schools should aim to extend children's knowledge of themselves and of the world in which they live, and through greater knowledge to develop skills and concepts, to help them relate to others, and to encourage a proper self-confidence. These aims are not necessarily identified with separate subject areas, nor allocated set amounts of time. Often a single activity promotes a variety of skills.*

The main purpose of primary schooling in Czechoslovakia *shall be to offer the base for a polytechnical education, to ensure intellectual development, a materialistic point of view, moral, aesthetic, physical and military preparation and preparation for secondary education.* For a more detailed presentation of the aims and objectives of primary education, reference can be made to the above-mentioned Volume 38 of the *International Yearbook of Education* (Unesco-IBE, 1986:114-31).

Another way to analyse the aims and objectives of primary education is to follow their nature, emphasis and change over a certain period of time. This is important for two main reasons. First, changes of aims and objectives may reflect new priorities for primary education as an expression of satisfaction or dissatisfaction with the old ones. Second, they may be a result of changes in the society at large where new demands, needs and expectations from the primary education system are called for. In both cases, information on past trends (prospects and failures) and on the projected future is vital to educational evaluation.

In Table 2 the major objectives of primary education in Nepal are shown over a long time period (pre-1951 to date). Many interesting trends in primary education can be observed from the Nepalese example. First, literacy remains a major objective of primary education over the entire period. Second, during the earlier periods, the aims and objectives of primary education were strictly related to different types of primary school (language schools, basic education schools and English-type schools). Third, during the post-1951 period, emphasis was given to the universalization of primary schooling following the recommendations of the Nepal National Education Planning Commission (NNEPC) in 1954 and that of the All Round National Education Committee (ARNEC) of 1961. Fourth, new objectives were set for primary education and greater emphasis was given to certain aspects of primary education at given periods of time. For example, during the period 1951-61, primary education for citizenship training, the development of a sense of loyalty to the crown and the country, the teaching of good manners and habits related to cleanliness and respect for elderly people were additional objectives for that level of education. Likewise, in the latest periods (1971-81 and 1981 to date), emphasis is given to the social and physical development of children in primary schools as components of their all-around development.

Table 2. Nepal: major objectives of primary education.

Pre - 1951 Period	1951 - 1961	1961 - 1971	1971 - 1981	1981 to date
Three types of schools A. Bhasha Pathsala (Language schools) - to impart knowledge about alphabet and numbers B. Basic education schools - to teach reading, writing and arithmetic - to integrate education and work C. English-type schools - to develop communication skills in English - to teach reading, writing and arithmetic - to provide general knowledge about history & geography	- to develop communication skills - to instil knowledge about health and hygiene - to develop appreciation of fine arts Recommendations of NNEPC - to eradicate illiteracy - to provide minimum fundamental education - to provide a foundation for higher education - to provide citizenship training - to contribute to nation-building	- to provide knowledge of science - to develop economic competency through vocational education - to develop aesthetic competencies Recommendations of ARNEC - to develop such habits as cleanliness and respect for older people - to develop loyalty to the crown and the country - to foster religious tolerance - to discourage use of drugs, alcohol, etc. - to engage in physical exercise and sport activities	- to impart literacy - to develop civic knowledge - to promote social and physical development - to develop scientific attitude Recommendations of NESP - to teach reading, writing and arithmetic - to provide general knowledge on Nepal - to develop loyalty to the King and the country - to provide instruction in an occupation such as agriculture	- to impart literacy - to develop a sense of devotion & loyalty to the country, king and god - to inculcate discipline and build character - to create interest in arts and crafts, and sports - to maintain physical and mental health

Source: adapted from CERID (1985:10).

The analysis presented in this section is not meant to examine aims and objectives that are specific to a given aspect of primary education, for instance, "equality of educational opportunity", "educational wastage", "scholastic achievement of primary school children", "quality of primary schooling", and so on. This is the subject of the remaining sections of this chapter and will be sufficiently covered in Chapter 5.

2.2 Evaluating primary education

The evaluation of primary education should in principle start with a detailed and systematic analysis of its aims and objectives. It should be clear to the evaluator or to the evaluation team whether such aims and objectives are policy-, plan-, programme- or project-based. As the foregoing discussion shows, objectives can be short-term, intermediate or long-term and can have different dimensions (political, social, economic, individual, national and universal). These are important concerns for educational evaluation as they determine the choice of indicators and criteria of success for a given policy, programme or project.

Who sets the criteria of success for an educational programme or project, how they are determined and for whose benefit are all pertinent evaluation questions. As Kidder and Judd (1987) have remarked, the criteria of success of given programmes are often not the same for the different groups concerned, (e.g. policy-makers, funding agencies, programme administrators and staff, and the clients themselves). Evaluation and evaluators are generally caught in a dilemma where "taking sides" becomes a necessity. None the less, it is important to note that evaluation is a common practice at primary as at other levels or types of education. The day-to-day monitoring of pupils' progress is a common type of classroom evaluations entrusted to teacher; national examinations at the end of the primary education cycle are another standard form of evaluation found in most education systems. In addition, there are evaluations which are tailored to the improvement, change or innovation of given educational programmes. They fall into the category of policy and programme-related evaluation. Comparisons of the merits or weaknesses of different curricula and syllabuses, teaching methods, training programmes for teachers and supervisors, tests and examinations, experimental or pilot programmes are cases in point. Likewise, an accumulated body of evaluation is found in the form of basic studies and research. Studies and research on the problems of educational wastage, poor scholastic achievement of pupils, disparities in educational performance along gender, socio-economic and regional lines are some examples.

While bearing in mind the diversity of policies, priorities, structures, content and methods of primary education systems, it is still possible to identify the major purposes of evaluation at this level of education. Evaluation may serve first and foremost the purpose of critically examining the general concerns of primary education. In this context, the overriding purpose of educational evaluation could be: (a) to provide diagnosis of the present and past development of primary education (achievements and failures); (b) to assess the future needs and means for primary education (the examination of future priorities and scenarios); (c) to study the resources available and earmarked for primary education (financial, human and material); and (d) to provide the type and quality of information required for decision-making, implementation and monitoring of primary education programmes and projects (data base, indicators, techniques).

The next step in primary education evaluation would require a focus on specific areas of intervention. Some of these areas are mentioned in the previous section, for example: access to and provision for to primary schooling; quality and relevance of primary schooling; educational wastage; cost and finance; and administration and management. Once the area of intervention is identified and the evaluation activity justified, it is possible to develop the appropriate and relevant evaluation designs and data-collection methods.

2.3 Evaluation designs for primary education

The progress achieved in the field of educational evaluation with respect to designs, techniques, data-collection procedures and so on is a rather recent development. In a recent work, *Educational Evaluation: The State of the Field* (Wolf, 1987), this progress is critically examined. For example, the article by Benson and Michael (1987:43-56) summarizes a twenty-year perspective of designing evaluation studies. The authors provide a systematic analysis of the purposes of different evaluation designs (experimental, quasi-experimental, survey and naturalistic designs) and their advantages and disadvantages for educational evaluation. Experimental, quasi-experimental and survey designs usually rely upon quantitative methods and techniques of evaluation while naturalistic designs go for the qualitative ones. A combination of both would strengthen the field of educational evaluation and would stand a better chance of affecting educational policies, plans, programmes and projects.

The previous chapter treated in greater detail some major theoretical, methodological and operational issues for evaluation, and for educational evaluation in particular. Most of these issues are of general relevance to the evaluation of programmes or projects at any level or type of education. In order to have a greater focus in the evaluation of primary education programmes, we have chosen to discuss evaluation designs in respect of two of the principal areas of primary education evaluation: first evaluation of quality of primary education and, second, evaluation of access to and opportunity for primary education. The latter is the major concern of Chapter 5 and is therefore not discussed here. The quality of primary schooling can be a vast area of inquiry. To provide an overview of suitable designs for the evaluation of this broad area, we have chosen to focus on the evaluation of primary school curriculum programmes. As there are many aspects of the curriculum that need to be evaluated, it is possible to arrive at a good platform for the presentation and discussion of different evaluation designs.

Primary school curriculum: use and application of different evaluation designs

In nearly all societies, the roles and functions assigned to primary education are constantly changing. Unfortunately, this has not led to corresponding successful changes in the system of primary education although there is an expressed concern about these changes. From the standpoint of curriculum, there is continuous pressure for greater improvement in the content of education and in the teaching-learning processes to meet and respond to individual and societal needs. Failure to adapt the curriculum to changes at individual and societal levels is partly a result of inborn contradictions and imbalances between old structures, content and methods and newly adopted objectives for primary education. Table 3 captures this issue in mapping out the problem, process and data for quality control of implemented curriculum over time. It also indicates the information required and the techniques that are more appropriate to: (a) identify the need for quality control; (b) find the cause of deterioration; and (c) apply corrective measures and investigate their effectiveness. In order that curriculum evaluation may contribute to quality improvement in primary education or education in general, the political climate for such evaluation should be present, the participatory role of the major actors and beneficiaries ensured, the design and methodologies appropriately chosen and, last but not least, necessary resources made available (see also Dahllöf, 1971; Lundgren, 1977).

Table 3. Quality control of implemented curriculum over time.

	1. Identify need for quality control	2. Find cause of deterioration	3. Apply corrective measures and investigate effectiveness
A. PROBLEM	Find out if an implemented curriculum continues to be effective Identify where quality control is needed	Understand why and how deterioration originated	Apply appropriate quality-control measures Find out whether a particular measure is effective
B. PROCESS	Compare student achievement data in the current term with those in the previous terms or years	Survey how the curriculum is implemented, under what conditions, to what student groups Analyse and compare a series of formative tests Derive hypotheses which explain why the effectiveness of the curriculum is decreasing	Organize appropriate quality-control measures Verify if these measures are effective under small-scale experimental situations Apply the verified quality-control measures to the target population
C. DATA	Summative assessment programmes or summative achievement tests administered every year End-of-course examinations Standardized achievement tests Expert and teacher judgement Attitude and interest survey Questionnaires Other unobtrusive measures	Formative tests School survey data Interviews & questionnaires Expert and teacher judgement Classroom observation	Formative and summative tests Attitude and interest survey Other unobtrusive measures

Source: adapted from Lewy (1977:154-5).

The evaluation of primary school curriculum should in principle involve the following:

An account of the extent to which the objectives of primary education are reflected in and implemented through the primary school curriculum (structure, content, method, organization and management).

A description and assessment of the relationship between programmes (quality, content and methods) for pre-service and in-service training of primary school teachers, inspectors, supervisors and those built-in or absent from the primary school curriculum.

An examination of the quality and relevance of teaching-learning materials (syllabuses, textbooks, teaching guides, etc.) from the standpoints of teaching and learning needs of teachers and pupils respectively.

A study of the appropriateness of teacher-learning techniques for given moments in teaching-learning processes and pupil-teacher interactions (memorization, experimental and exploratory exercises, group learning, questions and answers, classroom and homework assignments).

An examination of teaching-learning effectiveness (time allocations and uses for teaching and learning of given tasks and subjects; teacher-learner behaviours, attitudes and interactions; and performance of teachers and pupils).

One evaluation design cannot cope with all the possible questions raised in curriculum evaluation. The choice of the one or more designs would largely depend on the evaluation purpose or purposes, on the type of data required and on the audience or target groups benefiting from the evaluation. An experimental design will be more suitable for a programme where some impact evaluation is required. For example, any innovative programme should in principle not be implemented in the entire system of primary schooling before being tested (pre-test and post-test) on an experimental or pilot scheme. In the area of primary curriculum development, innovation or change, an experimental design can be used to evaluate, for instance: new training programmes for primary school teachers; new textbooks for certain primary school subjects; new syllabuses; or new teaching and learning equipment. Having a randomly chosen treatment group for the experimentation and a control group for comparison, the use of the experimental design permits an evaluation of the changes and relative effectiveness brought by the new programme in the classroom and during teaching-learning processes. If necessary, the experiment can be repeated several times either in the same setting or in other settings before any final evaluation of the possibility of its implementation on a national or sub-national scheme.

Some aspects of curriculum evaluation are better studied through the application of a quasi-experimental design as the focus is much more on the implementation aspects of the existing curriculum itself. Primary education curriculum implementation or the extent of it being successfully implemented depends upon internal as well as external factors. Henceforth, the evaluation design should accommodate the possibilities for mapping out both types of influences, which are sometimes determined by changes taking place inside and outside the classroom learning environments. In some quasi-experimental designs for educational evaluation, these changes are considered by the application of interrupted time-series designs (see Cook and Campbell, 1979). Having sound and reliable data on the programme at its initial (pre-test) stage and using a number of post-tests during the course of programme implementation to account for continuous feedbacks, the long-term effects of some elements in programme implementation can be ascertained. As Wolf (1987) has suggested, the principal advantage of quasi-experimental design for educational evaluation of programme implementation is that it can be replicated all along the implementation phase in different and specific settings, and as a result, the problem of non-randomization becomes less and less important. In this context, the quasi-experimental design can be used to evaluate the extent to which the primary school curriculum is implemented in accordance with curriculum plans and objectives and accounting for variations in school and classroom settings.

Many of the questions addressed in primary school curriculum evaluation require an extensive amount of data for both descriptive and explanatory purposes. Survey designs may serve such purposes. Through the application of different sampling techniques, these designs allow inferences to be made about the entire population. Having the possibility both of mapping the vast amount of information collected through questionnaires (structured and unstructured) and tests, and of making inferences about the population targeted from a sample or samples, survey designs are powerful tools for primary school curriculum evaluation. Questionnaires can be used to measure, for instance, the variations in classroom, school and local environmental settings in respect of the organization, management, content and application of the primary school curriculum. Data on the characteristics and behaviour of teachers and pupils, on classroom process variables, on school and home environments, and on the performance of teachers and pupils can all be analysed simultaneously to account for variations or disparities in primary school curriculum implementation in different settings. Having such powerful statistical packages for the social sciences as SPSS and SAS, these vast amounts of data can easily be processed and analysed for descriptive, exploratory and explanatory purposes. They can be analysed in various ways, i.e. from simple descriptive tables (means, frequencies, cross-tabulations and percentages) to complex multivariate statistics (correlations and regressions) suiting the different needs of the target audience (policy-makers, programme administrators and staff, funding agencies, educators and researchers).

The three evaluation designs discussed above do not enable the evaluator to act as a participant or observer in the actual teaching-learning processes. Participant observation belongs to the category of naturalistic designs where emphasis is given to the contextual situation of the programme under evaluation. Evaluators often forget to acknowledge that evaluation information of a qualitative nature gathered through participant observation, case-studies, documentary or content analysis of programmes, field notes and unstructured interviews is as important and reliable as the information gathered through quantitative methods. In the area of primary school curriculum evaluation, an evaluation design incorporating different types of classroom observation techniques will assist in in-depth evaluation of teaching-learning processes, pupil-teacher interactions, teachers' and pupils' time on tasks for given subjects, and so on. The evaluation of primary school curriculum sometimes calls for naturalistic designs which enable evaluators to collect in-depth descriptive, open-ended and narrative types of information on programme implementation. Chinapah and Fägerlind (1986) argue that the strength of naturalistic evaluation designs relies upon the quality of information collected and produced. Qualitative type of data on areas of programme implementation are not always available in conventional educational evaluation, for example, data on: (a) programme setting; (b) human and social interactions among various actors and beneficiaries and their different behaviours and attitudes; and (c) unintended actions or activities and unexpected outcomes. However, naturalistic evaluation designs have weaknesses just as the other designs do. Their main weaknesses lie in the area of reliability and validity of the data for making inferences about the targeted population. There are also several ethical issues to be considered, for example, the relationship between the observers and the observed (see Patton, 1980).

Space does not permit an in-depth examination here of the nature and application of the four designs in the evaluation of different educational programmes and projects at primary education level. As one can note, an evaluation design cannot be separated from theoretical, methodological and operational issues (Part One). Likewise, it is not meant for the evaluation of only one type of educational programme. We shall observe this in the discussion of the designs for evaluating literacy programmes and technical/vocational programmes in Chapters 3 and 4 respectively. The discussion in the coming chapters will broaden the debate on evaluation design initiated so far in this section.

2.4 Major parameters of primary education evaluation: sampling procedures, evaluation instruments and data management

We have repeatedly stressed that educational evaluation is an open area of inquiry where choices and compromises are to be made. A significant amount of work is usually necessary in the pre-planning, collection, processing and analysis of data and information for the evaluation of programmes and projects subjected to policy decisions, administration and implementation. The nature and scope of the data base as well as its quality, relevance, reliability and validity are pertinent questions for good-quality educational evaluation. In the evaluation of primary education programmes, several choices need to be made and these choices, in their turn, are conditioned by the nature of the evaluated programmes, the information required and the very purpose of evaluation itself. It is practically impossible to achieve all these without an operational framework incorporating the major parameters of educational evaluation. Such parameters are, for example, the sampling design, the choice of the unit or units of analysis, the selection of appropriate evaluation instruments and the methods of data management (collection, processing and analysis). It is only with an organized step-by-step operational framework that incongruence or imbalance at various phases of the evaluation can be avoided. In many developing countries, due to a lack of skilled personnel in educational evaluation, some important parameters are not respected and many evaluation activities are often stopped in progress and/or remain disorganized and unmanageable.

Sampling procedures

In the area of primary education, there are as many problems to be investigated as the number of schools. A systematic and comprehensive evaluation of primary schooling would most likely have to involve various actors (educational administrators, school head-teachers, teachers, pupils and parents) in the different stages of programme implementation. When an evaluation survey is required, it is necessary that all members of the defined target population have an equal chance or non-zero probability of being selected in the sample. In other types of evaluation, for instance, experimental and case-study types, additional sampling designs need to be made.

Sampling is a technique used to guarantee the equal representativeness of elements, groups, characteristics or strata of a target population in an evaluation survey. To carry out a successful evaluation of primary schooling, data representing the characteristics and processes of different environments of learning in the home and at school need to be collected. In order to capture the variations in these environments of learning, and also to ensure representativeness, the frequency distribution of element characteristics within the sample should be similar to the corresponding distributions within the target population (Ross, 1987:60). Once representativeness is guaranteed, it is possible to use inferential statistics to predict from one set of data to the target population. To ensure representativeness, the most common sampling designs are: (a) simple random sampling; (b) systematic sampling; (c) stratified proportionate or disproportionate sampling; and (d) cluster sampling. All four belong to the category of probability sampling. A brief description of these designs is given in Table 4. For certain primary education programmes (e.g. experimental and pilot programmes) generalizations to the entire primary school population are not necessary and in such contexts, non-probability samples (judgement sampling, convenience sampling, quota sampling, etc.) can be used. Sampling is a vast area and the subject of serious conceptual and methodological debate. For a more detailed discussion of these topics the reader is referred to Kish (1965), Babbie (1973) and Nachmias and Nachmias (1987).

Table 4. Description of four probability samples.

Types of sampling	Description
Simple random	Assign to each sampling unit a unique number; select sampling units by use of a table of random digits.
Systematic	Determine the sampling interval (N/n); select the first sample unit randomly; select remaining units according to interval.
Stratified proportionate	Determine strata; select from each stratum a random sample proportionate to the size of the strata in the population.
Stratified disproportionate	Determine strata; select from each stratum a random sample of the size dictated by analytical considerations.
Cluster	Determine the number of levels of clusters; from each level of clusters select randomly; ultimate units are groups.

Source: **Nachmias and Nachmias (1987:308).**

In many developing countries, in addition to the probability sampling designs mentioned above, it is important to include some major characteristics of the primary school system, namely: type of school (public or private); residential ecology (urban, semi-urban, rural) and size of school (large, medium, small). Reference can also be made to Chapter 5 for an example of a sampling design used to accommodate the major characteristics of the primary school system in Mauritius.

Evaluation instruments and data management

The development and construction of evaluation instruments demand, in the first place, a sound knowledge of the programme to be evaluated (its intended objectives, coverage, inputs, contents, implementation strategies and desired outputs). Second, any programme evaluation requires an in-depth literature review of the theory, research and findings related to the field under investigation in order to arrive at a conceptual framework or model guiding the development of the relevant instruments and data collection. Third, there is in fact a body of evaluation instruments (questionnaires - structured or unstructured; interviews - scheduled or unscheduled; criterion-referenced or norm-referenced tests; observation schedules, checklists, etc.) available for primary education evaluation. The choice depends upon a number of evaluation questions. Most of them were raised earlier. None the less, the choice depends largely on their suitability and cost-effectiveness with respect to the evaluated programme in question. Fourth, any type of instrument chosen calls for a certain method or methods of data collection (mailing, field administration, observation on sites, etc.). Finally, a structure for data management and analysis should be included during the entire evaluation exercise and not, as is often the case, considered the last aspect of educational evaluation. As will be shown in Chapter 5, all these steps are vital for primary education evaluation.

The evaluation of primary education in developing countries has for several years been influenced by the experience accrued from similar evaluation ventures in the more affluent societies, namely the developed industrialized countries. This has to a great extent influenced the development of evaluation instruments as well as the conceptual framework for primary education evaluation for developing countries (see Alexander and Simmons, 1975; Schiefelbein and Simmons, 1979; Heyneman and Loxley, 1982; Chinapah, 1983a; Nyström, 1985; Silanda, 1988). In his review of evaluation and research studies on primary education in developing countries, Chinapah (1983a:44) argues that "there has often been a lack of appropriate measurement instrument tapping school (and home) process variables as well as a lack of an appropriate conceptualization of school learning processes". Husén et al. (1978) have also observed similar weaknesses from the their review of thirty-two recent studies on the relationship between teacher training and student achievement in developing countries:

> Ultimately, future research should not be preoccupied with the question whether trained teachers make a difference, since that question has already been answered by cumulative research evidence. The question which remains unanswered is how and because of what qualities and in what contexts do teachers make a difference. Answers to these questions will make significant contributions to our understanding of the teacher-learner process generally, and in LDCs, and will help improve schooling outcomes in a manner congruent with LDC needs. (Husén et al., 1978:47.)

Questionnaires can be used to capture the vast amount of information on home and school environments of learning (characteristics and process variables) and cognitive tests for the measurement of scholastic achievement at primary education level while other instruments such as interviews, observation schedules, periodic reports and checklists can focus on performance indicators at different levels (classroom, school, district, region, etc.). Reference can also be made to the work of Johnstone (1981) *Indicators of Education Systems* (see "Information Base for Evaluation" in Chapter 1). Data on the performance of the primary school system as a whole are just as important as data on pupils' scholastic achievement. A primary evaluation model may consist of the following performance indicators: (a) survival, repeater, dropout, retention and flow rates; (b) class sizes, hours (lessons) per class; (c) pupil/teacher ratio, structure in teaching staff (tenure), teaching norms, average audience, teachers' average teaching load; (d) wages, overheads; and (e) survival rates for tenures, procedure of promotion.

Data management (collection, processing and analysis) is sometimes regarded as the most painstaking, costly, lengthy and complex phase of educational evaluation. Good-quality, well-designed educational evaluation would avoid many of these problems if pre-testing and pilot studies are carried out prior to the main evaluation study. Pre-testing involves initial testing of the major aspects of the evaluation parameters (instruments, sampling, data-collection methods, and programmes for data analysis) while pilot studies are "miniaturized walkthroughs of the entire study" (Babbie, 1973:205). Due to time and resource constraints, however, many primary education evaluation activities attribute secondary importance to pre-testing and pilot studies. In our example in Chapter 5, the contrary will be witnessed as without pre-testing and pilot studies, it would have been impossible to develop appropriate instruments and select appropriate methods of data collection. The actors in this evaluation consisted of a majority of primary school pupils with a poor command of the English language, poorly educated parents and field researchers with hardly any prior training in questionnaires and test administration. Most of these difficulties were observed during pre-testing and pilot studies and the necessary adjustments were made and appropriate solutions found.

It has been a common practice to collect as much data as possible through the application of all existing evaluation methods and instruments in the evaluation of primary education in developing countries, partly as a result of improper directives given to educational evaluation and partly because of the poor level of competencies and skills of evaluators. In their evaluation of the nation-wide assessment of quality of education in Ethiopia, Tung and Chinapah (1985) stress these weaknesses. During the later phase of data management (capture, file building and data analysis) the following problems arose:

> It was not very clear which types of data sets would require computer facilities and which would need simple techniques using calculators. The linkage between the stages of instrument construction and data analysis was not properly understood... (L)ocal facilities (expertise, computer programmes, and computer time) could not cope with the volume of data sets involved. In the data analysis stage, very little attention was given to the analysis of qualitative data. The pressure for quick

computable results and the lack of competence and skills limited the scope for using qualitative methods in the data analysis (e.g. field reports from in-depth interviews and observations, content analysis of curriculum programmes, case-study narratives and the like). (Tung and Chinapah, 1985:6-7.)

We shall conclude this chapter with a few remarks concerning the various phases in the evaluation of primary education programmes and projects. First, the objectives of primary education should be properly analysed using, for instance, policy-analysis methods. These objectives, once properly defined in operational terms for primary education evaluation, should serve as a point of departure in planning and implementing the various evaluation phases. Second, distinctions are to be made between various evaluation designs in terms of their specific and complementary roles. These distinctions would facilitate the choice of appropriate instruments, sampling designs, data-collection and data-analysis methods. Third, primary education evaluation or any type of educational evaluation should include, at a very early stage, a review of the literature (theory, concepts, empirical evidence, evaluation techniques, etc.). Fourth, pre-testing and pilot studies should be encouraged prior to the main evaluation activity. Fifth, instruments as well as items should always be related to the evaluation objectives as viewed from the standpoints of programme objectives, structure, coverage, content and strategies for implementation. Sixth, there is always a need for a trade-off between the qualitative and the quantitative aspects of the information base of educational evaluation if correct and timely answers are to be given to the target audience (policy-makers, programme administrators, front-line implementors and beneficiaries). Finally, no good-quality primary education evaluation can be ensured in the absence of a climate (political, bureaucratic, socio-cultural and pedagogical) where conflicts and compromises are accepted and tolerated; where participation from all those concerned in decision-making and programme implementation is ensured; and where a mechanism for continuous evaluation or built-in process evaluation is maintained and made operational.

A great deal of what has been said in this chapter may serve as feedback to our presentation and discussion of the evaluation of literacy programmes in Chapter 3. However, it is important to note that the nature and coverage of literacy programmes call for additional evaluation considerations. Here, it is imperative to consider: (a) the wide range of objectives of these programmes; (b) their cross-sectoral nature (i.e. in relation to health, family planning, nutrition and productivity); and (c) their immediate and long-term outcomes. The evaluation of literacy programmes demands greater efforts from the standpoints of information collection, processing and analysis. Likewise, there seems to be a greater need for a "mix" of evaluation designs and techniques.

3. The evaluation of literacy programmes

3.1 Aims and objectives of literacy programmes

Attempting to conceptualize the literacy situation in a world in which nearly one-third of the population are illiterate is difficult. One person might argue that great progress has and continues to be made, while another might see the same data and come to the pessimistic realization that we are losing the hopeless struggle to eradicate widespread illiteracy. Both would be right. The total number of illiterate persons continues to increase as the population swells, especially in the developing countries. However, the number of people being reached through literacy campaigns and ever-expanding education networks is also increasing. Further, the overall percentage of illiterate persons is decreasing.

There are several reasons for the constant high rate of illiteracy, even in the face of the enormous attention it has received. They include: (a) rapid population growth; (b) the failure to universalize primary education, regardless of stated policy objectives; (c) low priority given to literacy activities; and (d) limited financial and skilled human resources. None the less, such claims as these are hard to assess, for in the Third World itself, there are many troublesome conditions that can hinder evaluation efforts of in the field of literacy. Beyond the extensive financial crisis, the many languages and cultural groupings brought together by colonial pasts can complicate efforts. Further the infrastructure upon which to construct, and later assess, literacy is not always present.

What this indicates is that while the means and methods of the past have been effective, much more will be required to deal with the problem of illiteracy in the future. New schemes are needed to make better use of the decreasing resources available. Alternative frameworks and planning are needed. This is where evaluation can play an important role. However, there is still much growth needed concerning the methodology of evaluation, especially within the complex setting of literacy evaluation. In referring to literacy, it is important to note that we are referring to functional literacy, which nearly all programmes now pursue. The definition of literacy, as conceived in various literacy programmes, is almost invariably described in terms that go beyond the 3 R's, and include knowledge, skills and attitudes conducive to the enhancement of the quality of life. Functional literacy attempts to do more than teach reading, writing and basic numeracy. It also attempts to teach those involved how to play a more effective role in their socio-economic and political environments. Of course, the precise definition of literacy must vary according to time and place, but what needs to be emphasized here is the ability to function effectively in one's own society. Functional literacy is more than a set of skills; it is also the ability to apply them.

As pointed out in Chapter 1, the definition of aims and objectives is the most important part of an evaluation's first stage. The objectives must be clearly defined, if possible in quantified terms. This may involve a review of official documents, consultation with responsible persons such as administrators and technicians and the consideration of expert advice. It may also involve collecting and recruiting relevant information concerning the participants and their environment. Aims and objectives can often be seen as the connection between the initial situation of participants and their environment, and the desired point of completion, which is often embodied in the goals of those planning the programme. Thus, the formulation of aims and objectives should follow after and reflect the assessment of literacy needs. Further, the objectives of a literacy programme should consider other sectors such as health, agriculture, environment and culture. Some general examples of literacy objectives include the following: (a) remove a means of exploitation; (b) develop the economy and individuals and help them grow; (c) promote modernization; (d) promote nation-building, communication and cohesion; (e) protect cultural identity and political independence; (f) promote democratic participation; and (g) facilitate the mobilization of human and natural resources.

The aims and objectives of a literacy programme depend largely upon the approach taken. While there are various approaches to literacy (many which define themselves by their differing methods), these can generally be grouped into two contrasting approaches that deal specifically with literacy. They are the selective intensive approach and the literacy campaign. The approach chosen will reflect the context and nature of the literacy problem and resources available, as well as the ideological inclinations of the state. The selective intensive approach can be characterized by its emphasis on functional literacy; it is also the more traditional of the two approaches mentioned here. The Experimental World Literacy Programme (EWLP), conducted between 1967 and 1973, was basically a selective intensive effort to combat illiteracy in eleven different developing countries. This programme - and especially the assessments which followed - have provided much information, experience, a base for further efforts of its kind and extensive rationalizations for efforts not of its kind.

The aims and objectives of literacy programmes should be broad and far-reaching, but still realistic and achievable. Confusing goals and targets must be guarded against. But these very aims and objectives depend also upon the type of education (formal, non-formal or informal) used and the age-group targeted. Literacy itself is one of the main objectives within the formal education system. However, for various reasons, formal education is not available for all, or else it proves ineffective at providing a quality education for those enrolled. The formulation of objectives is an important part of planning, and must be done with a clear vision of the targets of literacy as it concerns both the individuals involved and the society at large. Hamadache and Martin (1988:69) point out three basic elements concerning planning and objectives which became obvious from the analysis of the EWLP:

1. A functional programme must first of all be organized with an economic and/or social and/or cultural objective in view and should be the direct instrument for its achievement.
2. The socio-cultural milieu concerned by the operations prepared in this way must participate in the design and implementation of the programme.
3. The acquisition of reading, writing and arithmetic must be seen as a means of achieving the objective and ensuring the participation of the milieu.

The definition of what literacy means varies from place to place and from time to time. A broader definition of literacy requires broader objectives to include involvement and development of the socio-economic arena, and the safeguarding of cultural identity and national interests. As literacy is very closely related to socio-economic and cultural planning, the objectives of literacy must also be considered in light of this relationship. Further, in order to achieve the objectives of literacy, the planning process must consider the socio-economic and cultural milieu, and plan to make the best possible use of them. This may mean setting objectives that coincide with these forces.

As most large-scale literacy programmes are orchestrated by the national government, it is important to consider the state objectives. Lind (1988:14) has identified three principal state objectives of literacy:

> socio-political objectives (such as nation-state formation, participation in on-going transformations, mobilization in support of a new regime), which are often the driving force behind mass literacy campaigns; economic objectives, promoting a process of gradual improvement of living standards, which can either result in selective work-oriented programmes within specific development projects or in a more general programme as one of several inputs to building economic growth; and general socio-economic objectives, often in a context of relatively low priority to literacy, where provision is made through state services in response to public and/or international demand.

One important area concerning literacy programmes that we shall mention in passing concerns the post-literacy objectives. The objectives of post-literacy programmes usually consider the retention of reading, writing and numeracy, which enables the learners to function effectively in their everyday lives. Also included within these objectives is the provision of further educational programmes, both formal and informal, which help those who wish to continue their education to do so.

3.2 Scope and coverage

Extensive illiteracy remains essentially a political problem compounded by economic and social factors. It is a problem most evident in developing countries, but is increasingly being seen in some industrialized countries. Within particular groupings illiteracy is most prevalent among females, the poor and ethnic minorities. Overall, illiteracy represents a hindrance to development and should be considered in both its national and international context. Thus, any evaluation of literacy efforts can and should likewise span these two contexts.

In evaluating the success of a literacy programme, we must critically examine its use of resources. We must also consider how the impact of literacy efforts affects other areas and sectors, such as health, fertility and productivity. The impact of a literacy programme can reach much further than a statistic relating to the ability to read and write; thus, the evaluation of literacy is complicated. Many interlinked impacts can spell out efficient and effective programming. The challenge of a literacy evaluation is to piece together and decipher these various impacts.

Literacy has a broad impact, both within the academic milieu and within the economic, social and political spheres; thus it is very difficult to assess. This difficulty is compounded by the fact that much of literacy's impact is long-term and cannot be assessed immediately after the programme's conclusion. Some impacts of evaluation take years to surface. Unfortunately, many evaluations are planned and allocated resources for a short period of time. If an evaluation is to assess the impact of a literacy programme on the political or economic development of the immediate region or the country at large, the scope for the evaluation will be very wide. The practical boundaries of the evaluation will, however, be largely determined by the objectives of the literacy campaign.

In planning literacy efforts, a few trends must be considered which complicate the planning and implementation of literacy programmes. One is that in many developing countries, the actual numbers of illiterate persons are increasing. Another is that the available resources for the education sector and extra-educational activities are decreasing. But from crisis often comes opportunity. We can look at the efforts that have succeeded in the face of these adverse circumstances and learn from them.

The case of Ethiopia, highlighted in Chapter 6, perhaps represents one of the better examples, especially in light of all the obstacles it faced.

The scope of a particular evaluation will vary according to the scope of the literacy programme itself, the type of information sought and the instruments utilized. While it may not be possible to complete qualitative questionnaires or conduct interviews with every participant in a literacy programme, it is relatively easy to collect basic background data on each participant, as well as general test scores and classroom data which each instructor can collect and channel to the evaluation team. If a project is of limited scope or coverage, evaluation may not be necessary; resources may not allow this.

In a formative evaluation, where monitoring and the supplying of feedback for implementation improvement play a major role, there are a number of relevant elements of the literacy programme that could be covered, depending on the scope of the evaluation. A suggested list of these might include the following (Unesco, 1982b:5):

Programme setting. The existence of: (a) an appropriate administration structure; (b) active community participation; (c) linkages with community development agencies and activities; (d) linkages with formal education; and (e) provision for professional support.

Finances. Availability as planned (amount and timing).

The learners. Data regarding: (a) the number enrolled and their composition, especially with reference to the representation of disadvantaged groups; (b) attendance, repetition, completion of course, time taken to complete course; and (c) test/examination results, if any.

The instructors. Data regarding their: (a) number; (b) method of recruitment; (c) orientation/training and experience; (d) categories, e.g. paid or volunteer; drawn from the community or outside; (e) attendance; and (f) participation in community activities.

Instructional materials. Whether developed according to plan (it is presumed that the plan provides relevance and variety).

Teaching. Number of lessons observed by monitoring personnel, and general impression.

Logistics. The availability of: (a) classrooms; (b) lighting (fuel, lamps); (c) instructional materials in time and in adequate number; and (d) chalk and other supplies.

Congruence of mass media messages. The extent to which the mass media (newspapers, radio) reinforce or diverge from the messages conveyed by the programme.

Outputs. The percentage: (a) completing programmes successfully; (b) enrolling for new programmes; (c) reported as making use of the knowledge and insights given by the programme; and (d) actively engaged in continuing literacy (in this connection an assessment of the continuing supply of post-literacy materials to reading rooms and libraries is also important).

3.3 The evaluation objectives

Within a situation of limited social spending, literacy must confirm its role in development and positive social change in order to compete for resources. Thus, one of the important objectives of a literacy evaluation is to assess the cost-benefit relationship of the programme, the aim here being to increase the efficiency and effectiveness of literacy planning. Later, when literacy programmes are under way, there is a need to verify that the programmes are meeting their stated objectives. In both cases evaluation is crucial.

Of course, in a general sense, one cannot simply draw up a common list of evaluation objectives for a literacy programme. First, literacy programmes can differ drastically (as has been pointed out in the first two sections of this chapter). Second, evaluations vary widely. Thus, rather than attempt to draw up a general list of literacy evaluation objectives, we shall name the main influences and factors which order them. Some of these are as follows: (a) the nature and approach of the literacy programme itself; (b) the scope and coverage of the literacy programme; (c) the type of evaluation (formative, summative or comprehensive); (d) the design of the evaluation; (e) the purpose of the evaluation; and (f) the funders and the intended audience of the evaluation information. This is only a suggested list; however, it shows out clearly just how closely interrelated the various components and elements of a literacy programme and its evaluation are.

As was made clear earlier, evaluation should ideally be conducted in parallel with the project or programme cycle. It should begin with the initial assessment of literacy needs and continue through and extend beyond the termination of the project or programme. In its initial stage, evaluation should determine some particular aspects of the programme in question, such as: (a) its need; (b) its specific objectives; (c) its potential acceptability; and (d) its administrative and financial feasibility. During the implementation of a literacy programme, the evaluation can serve to identify the strengths and weaknesses in design and operation, and in light of these, suggest ways and means to improve the programme. In this capacity, the assessment activities are referred to as formative evaluation.

In order to conduct a thorough summative evaluation, data concerning the knowledge, skills and attitudes of the learners must be collected before the programme begins. After the intervention has ended, new data collected can be compared, and the extent of change measured. It is often necessary to re-evaluate the programme's impact at a later time, since the data and information regarding the impact are inadequate for assessing the stated objectives of the literacy programme which often refer to long-term impacts. Unfortunately, practical evaluation situations seldom allow adequate time to assess these impacts, instead focusing on immediate numbers and figures at hand.

One general warning concerning the objectives for a literacy evaluation is that these objectives are often too broad in nature and are not properly defined. This situation can have the following results during the implementation stages: (a) a vast amount of data collected; (b) all possible methods of data collection utilized; and (c) many invalid responses, as well as a quantity of unreliable information and duplicated items. In the first phase of the literacy evaluation in Ethiopia (see Chapter 6) some of these very difficulties were encountered.

3.4 Choice of evaluation designs

The evaluation of a literacy programme, like any other type of evaluation, must have a design. Both experimental and quasi-experimental designs have been used in literacy evaluations. Today, however, there has been more emphasis on evaluation developing its own designs, since the applied nature of evaluation is very different from the controlled experimental setting.

The evaluation design will of course reflect the approach undertaken. While we are often preoccupied with the traditional or classical approach to evaluation (which is considered to be more objective and scientific), there remain other approaches such as the holistic and participative approaches to evaluation. Bhola (1979) refers to three current approaches to evaluation: participative, naturalistic and bureaucratic. To these three approaches he adds another, called the situation-specific strategy model, which is a more comprehensive and integrated approach to making evaluation operational within functional literacy programmes and projects. It deals with all aspects of evaluation from the design of evaluation policies to the making of necessary tools and instruments for data collection, and it even considers the use of data in decision-making. This situation-specific strategy is inclusive of all three previously mentioned models and approaches.

There are five stages in the development of the situation-specific strategy:

> (1) ordering the world of evaluation and change by conceiving it in terms of systems and networks; (2) articulating the means-ends relationships implicit in the change programme to clarify the strategy of change; (3) generating profiles of information needs and evaluation issues through the interaction of the system and the strategy of change; (4) developing a situation-specific strategy agenda for a particular programme at a particular place and time; and (5) choosing methodologies and techniques that are technically appropriate and situationally feasible. (Bhola, 1979:33.)

An evaluation's research design must single out the choice of instruments, data and analyses that must be accounted for early in the study. The variables we are concerned with in literacy programmes are difficult to control. Thus, the design of the evaluation and the choice of techniques and instruments to be used should be undertaken carefully and stringently. There are several elements of design, such as sampling, matching and control groups (see Chapter 1), which will not be developed here; however, it should be emphasized that a good design is very important as it will provide helpful and valid information for decision-makers and others involved.

If possible, the instruments developed should be tested on a pilot-study basis prior to their full-scale application. It is here that many shortcomings of the instruments can be detected, for example, problems with clarity, format (depth and breadth), objectivity and reliability. Instrument construction should be closely linked to the data-analysis phase. Literature reviews should also be carried out prior to the development of instruments. Such reviews can reduce the vast amount of unreliable items in the different sets of instruments.

Concerning the monitoring role of evaluation, we shall list some generally recognized instruments which can be employed by an evaluation design (Unesco, 1982b:27):
1. Survey schedule for identification of potential learners, their needs and the availability of resources locally.
2. Instructor's diary and/or attendance register of learners.
3. Instructor's initial report to the supervisor or to the official to whom he/she is accountable.
4. Instructor's periodic returns.
5. Instructor's final return, highlighting the outcome of the course.
6. Supervisor's diary containing observations and notes recorded during his/her visits to the classes and also comments on the returns received from the instructors.
7. Supervisor's periodic report to the district office.
8. Supervisor's data register.
9. District officer's periodic returns to the national headquarters.
10. District officer's data register.
11. Provincial officer's returns to the national headquarters.
12. Provincial officer's data register.
13. National level register.
14. Annual report on the programme.

The above list is an aggregate list and not a representative one. None the less, such examples as these should prove helpful in envisaging the actual design and implementation of a literacy programme evaluation. Chapter 6 will return to these matters as it provides an overview of the Ethiopian Literacy Campaign Evaluation.

3.5 Choice of indicators and variables

As is typical in the social sciences, all the variables - and often the most important ones - cannot be easily measured as they are impossible to isolate and control completely. Examples of these include changes in attitude and behaviour. Variables are used for measurement and because of their variations they reflect an evolving or changing situation. The evaluator should describe, analyse and seek explanations from these variances. At the same time, change is hard to measure objectively without indicators which are attached to human and social conditions. However, one must be cautious with indicators as they can sometimes be attached in an arbitrary or invalid fashion.

For a literacy project, the variables should concern the participants, facilities and materials available, and the results of tests or classroom assessments (there are of course many other variables that one could be concerned with). These variables should be measured at the beginning and conclusion of a project as well as at other points in time deemed to be critical. The findings can then be presented in descriptive charts and await further analysis. The data collected for the variables, both before and after, can reveal many things (for example, the dropout rate) and they allow easy comparison from site to site. These data, if collected at stages throughout the intervention, can provide effective information to help make adjustments during implementation. If one project is performed particularly well, project managers from other sites can learn from it. Problems that arise can be pinpointed early, remedial action taken and satisfactory progress maintained.

The indicators and variables chosen will, of course, reflect the nature of the evaluation. For example, if the evaluation is intended for monitoring purposes, such critical indicators as the following might be considered: rate of participation; content and presentation of teaching materials; teaching methods; organization of the programme; recruitment and training of teachers; ratio of dropouts; ratio of attendance; ratio of registration per programme; and ratio of time utilization. In developing the indicators and selected variables for use in an evaluation, the evaluation team should seek inputs from all involved and they should attempt to make them objective and theoretically sound. To ensure the validity of an indicator, it may be desirable to draw up other indicators of the same condition being measured.

The following list of indicators (as adapted from Bhola, 1979:57) which were selected and used in the EWLP can be helpful in better illustrating the nature and application of indicators. This list includes both minimum and recommended indicators.

Basic statistical indicators
Quantitative aspects
1. Ratio of inscription in programme: indicator is a ratio between the number of participants originally registered and the number of places available.
2. Rate of dropouts.
3. Rate of attendance.
4. Time utilization: indicator is a ratio between class sessions planned and actually held.
5. Rate of coverage: indicator is a ratio between number of eligible clients and those actually covered in a programme.
6. Rate of participation in final tests.

Qualitative aspects
1. Literacy acquisition.
2. Acquisition of technical and professional knowledge.
3. Acquisition of knowledge of a socio-economic character.

Degree of adoption of writing, reading and calculating
1. Use of writing ability.
2. Use of reading ability.
3. Use of arithmetical ability.

Indicators pertaining to economic growth and development
Production
1. Increase in production per capita.
2. Quality of products.
3. Selling price.
4. Price (per quantitative unit) of the elements entering cost of production.

Income - living standards
1. Increase in the number of durable goods and improvements contributing to the standard of living.
2. Increase of net global monetary income of individuals.

Production, servicing and transport equipment
1. Increase in equipment for production, servicing or transport (in programmes for small agricultural producers).

Socio-economic attitudes
1. Importance of changes in the domain of socio-economic attitudes and in the individual's role in society.

Attitudes towards education
1. Rate of scholarization of participants' children: this is a ratio between the total number of children of school age and those actually attending school.
2. Rate of interruption of schooling in participants' children: this is a ratio between the number of participants' children

who interrupted their schooling and of interruptions in the total school-going population.

Professional competence
1. Adoption rate of recommended innovations.
2. Level of know-how in the fields covered by the programme.
3. Increase in desire for changes and technical innovations.

Relation towards means of mass communication
1. Ownership of radios and television sets.
2. Preference for educational programmes.

Health, hygiene and safety
1. Acquisition of knowledge of health, hygiene and safety around the home.
2. Acquisition of knowledge of health, hygiene and safety in work settings.

Costs and cost-benefit analysis
1. Per capita cost of functional literacy.

These indicators reflect the objectives of the EWLP. Of course, objectives vary greatly from programme to programme; thus these indicators are only suggestions, and are included here to help the reader better envision the realm and possibilities of indicators appropriate to literacy evaluations. Bhola (1979) himself has pointed out that many of these indicators are not themselves directly observable, and will need to be defined in other more specific indicators which can be measured.

3.6 Data-collection procedures and data analysis

Data collection must be carefully planned. The choice of variables and indicators will largely determine the data to be collected and will reflect the focus and scope of the assessment. The data collected from the various instruments can be organized, processed and manipulated by means of pen and paper, card sorters and/or computers. Today, most of the data analysis is dealt with on computers. None the less, the evaluator should keep in mind the extensive documentation (the thousands of figures to be considered, sorted and categorized, and the hundreds of calculations) involved with each variable selected. Thus, the variables should be chosen only after careful consideration of the means and resources available for the evaluation. The Ethiopian Literacy Campaign Evaluation ran into such problems early on (see Chapter 6), as much data was gathered on variables which were later not taken into consideration.

Merely noting differences when comparing data is not necessarily sufficient to allow claims that such differences exist. Further evidence is often needed and can be provided with statistical analysis. This involves the calculation of averages of series and variances, and the submission of results to other statistical tests, such as variance analysis. In further analysis of differences, it is possible to reapply the tests, taking into account the characteristics of the variables. The results may then point to the reasons for the differences, such as sex, age, socio-economic status, or even the time and place of the literacy course.

The types and categories of data that could be collected concerning a literacy programme are enormous. It is important to distinguish early on the data to be collected and focus on them. The data collected will also reflect the purpose of the evaluation. If the evaluation is formative, and intended to provide feedback to improve implementation, the required data will differ drastically from a summative evaluation, which will assess the programme's overall outcome and effectiveness.

Couvert (1979) outlines three areas or tasks of data analysis: descriptive, comparative and explanatory. The descriptive task may be accomplished with surveys of the milieu and descriptive statistical tables of the data collected. Such a task permits the classification of groups concerned; however it would probably not provide information necessary to determine significant differences. Simple statistical tests applied to the described data can provide much of the information necessary for comparison, i.e. averages, frequencies and variances. The task of explanation will usually be dealt with on the basis of simple hypotheses or explanatory theoretical models that are applied and then verified or disproved by the collected and analysed data.

Evaluating literacy programmes is as complex as evaluating programmes in the area of technical/vocational education. The latter is the subject of our presentation and discussion in Chapter 4. This complexity has much to do with the nature, scope, domain and depth of these programmes. In the evaluation of technical/vocational programmes, there is often the need to combine different evaluation methods and techniques. Chapter 4 demonstrates how such a combination is vital for the evaluation of different components of technical/vocational education, for example, programme content, logistics component, personnel component and programme performance.

4. The evaluation of technical/vocational education

4.1 Aims and objectives of technical/vocational education

There has been much discussion as to whether vocational and vocationalization are new terms for an old phenomenon or not. Yet, since the appearance of formal schooling, schools throughout the world have provided some type of training for manual work, as well as the learning of practical and productive tasks (see also Gustafsson, 1987). After the Second World War, however, formal schooling took a more academic and theoretical direction.

At the time of independence for many Third World nations, and during the decade that followed, it was clear that the schools produced pupils who could not find jobs at all, let alone appropriate jobs. Then, during the 1960s vocationalization and diversification (of secondary education) became themes in the development plans of many countries as they attempted to adjust schooling more closely to the needs and demands of the labour market. The vocationalization of secondary education refers to curriculum change in a practical or vocational direction (Lauglo and Lillis, 1988).

It was believed that all types of technical/vocational education should have labour-market relevance, as it helped to make all students employable and transmitted skills that were useful in the labour market. The purpose of the vocationalization effort was from the beginning to train the manpower that was needed in the starting - or coming - industrialization process of many developing countries.

It is important to spell out the aims and objectives of technical/vocational education as the trend towards vocationalization grows and evolves internationally. One of the major aims of curriculum diversification has been the transmitting of skills and attitudes which will be useful in gaining jobs. The trend is moving academic curricula closer to the realm of vocational relevance. In many developing countries this also means the generation of favourable attitudes for living and working in rural areas, as well as preparation for self-employment (Lauglo and Lillis, 1988).

The goals and rationales of vocationalization are often related to and influenced by ideals of: (a) general education; (b) political ideologies; and (c) economic relevance. Generally speaking, the aims and objectives of technical/vocational education in the Third World countries had more or less the following formulation during the first phase: (a) to provide well-defined specialized skills; (b) to stop the exodus to the urban centres; and (c) to change the attitudes (of the students) to manual labour. (Hultin, 1986.)

The objectives or goals subsequently changed and came to have the following formulations (Lillis and Hogan as cited in Hultin, 1986): (a) alleviate unemployment; (b) reorient student attitudes towards rural society; (c) halt urban migration; and (d) transmit skills and attitudes that were useful in employment.

The objectives have changed still further, as they attempt to meet the needs and demands in today's fast-changing information and technology society. In addition, egalitarian aims have been introduced for technical/vocational education. It should not only provide lower-school performers or underprivileged categories of people with the skills that are useful in the labour market, but also encourage those performing well in the school and the more privileged to engage in technical/vocational or manual work and not only in white-collar occupations (Lauglo and Lillis, 1988).

Vocationalization can take many forms. It could represent a separate institution away from the academic schools. These institutions are often referred to as technical/vocational schools. Alternatively, it can be established within the mainstream secondary schools as a compulsory or optional subject. This is then usually referred to as Industrial Education (IE), and is often pre-vocational as it does not develop completely the required skills and experience for entry into a technical occupation. (While there is not a clear distinction between vocational and pre-vocational training, the latter's goals are generally less understood, and it is assumed that further job training is required.) This differentiation between vocational and pre-vocational meant that some education was more specialized and some more general in character. The former was to provide the labour market with highly specialized manpower, while the latter was intended merely to create a disposition for a more positive attitude towards technical and manual work.

Technical/vocational education can be more problematic to evaluate than general education for several reasons. It is supposed to produce specific competencies and knowledge that are directly and visibly applicable in society. Thus, this implies that the evaluation of technical/vocational education might be a harder task than evaluation of primary education, for example. It is important to remember that the criteria and specifics of an evaluation will depend largely on the objectives of the technical/vocational programme or project in question. It may be difficult to identify these objectives as there may often be multiple and conflicting ones. A further difficulty in evaluating technical/vocational education can be highlighted by its common, but vague, objective to alleviate youth unemployment and to assist school-leavers to move directly into jobs or self-employment in a relevant sector. How can this objective be assessed when it is threatened by widespread unemployment, especially for young people?

4.2 The programme setting

Within its various settings, we find vocational training ranging from learning about production without contact with - or participation in - the labour market, to learning in production with principally apprenticeship participation in productive tasks. But which is the most effective and fruitful setting for technical/vocational training? Hultin (1986) has made an overview of a large number of evaluation studies of vocational education in developing countries. He found that vocational and technical schools were reported to do well in middle-income developing countries, while they faced problems in low-income LDCs, particularly in Africa. However, most evaluations have been conducted so early after completion that little is known about the employment of school graduates.

According to Lauglo and Lillis (1988), vocational education might be of the following types: (a) pre-vocational education (preparation for vocational training); (b) skills training streamed into general education; and (c) principally skills training for direct entry into jobs.

It may be of use at this point to review briefly the nature of projects and programmes, especially as they relate to technical/vocational training. A project is a particular set of goals to be achieved, and the set of human, economic and other resources which are utilized in order to attain these goals as well as the activities that are performed in this direction. A programme is a comprehensive and extended project or a set of interrelated smaller projects. (More has been said on this topic in Chapter 1).

A programme or a project may vary in scope, domain and depth. The scope refers broadly to: (a) the duration in time; and/or (b) the extension socially, economically, geographically, etc.; and/or (c) the number of domains involved. An example of a technical/vocational education programme might be the nationwide introduction of an industrial branch in the secondary schools of a country; such a programme would have a wide scope but would cover an intermediate number of domains (secondary education, vocational training, a certain number of enterprises, etc.). Thus, a domain refers to a specific policy area. Depth refers to the degree to which deeper cultural values of the target populations are concerned. Normally, a programme of the above mentioned type does not have much depth, while an agricultural programme in a Third World country may go into much greater depth.

Every programme is introduced and implemented in a particular environment but, first, some important contextual aspects should be mentioned. During the phase prior to the implementation of a programme into its environment, the setting has to be carefully explored and studied. This setting has various aspects which include: (a) the international setting; (b) the national setting, which includes (i) the political system; (ii) the economic system; (iii) the cultural pattern; and (iv) the administrative system. The evaluation study - whether it takes place continuously during the project period from the planning phase onwards, or is made as an ex-post evaluation - should take all these aspects into consideration.

Another consideration related to the overall environment is the role of international agencies which have an influence upon development projects and programmes. In some cases, the influence from the international agencies has directed the programmes and projects more towards forgotten groups (such as women and rural populations), and sometimes projects may take a more advanced or urban form than the national authorities intended from the beginning. Yet there are other ways in which they might influence educational programmes. For example, we may want to consider the following:

They may suggest particular studies or analyses (of the labour market, for example), and the results of these studies may then make the national authorities initiate certain projects, which they would not yet have started without the newly produced knowledge.

The international agencies themselves may suggest certain projects.

The national authorities may have some ideas or plans and demand economic aid. The international agencies may then require that certain conditions are fulfilled before they provide the economic resources that are demanded.

In an overview of evaluations of World Bank-supported projects in the area of technical/vocational education, Hultin (1986) found that most of the projects were biased. For example, the training needs of the large non-formal economic sector had not been covered and women had often been overlooked. Whether this is due to the international influence or not is impossible to judge but it should be kept in mind when evaluation studies are conducted.

It is safe to say that schools will differ greatly in their technical/vocational climate or atmosphere. The society, which largely forms this atmosphere, must be considered when planning or evaluating technical/vocational education. How supportive and ready is the society? Do the values of the community and the planned intervention mesh or clash? In an International Institute for Educational Planning (IIEP) document certain factors concerning the society at large are mentioned in relation to the implementation of educational programmes and projects. Thus, an evaluation study of an educational programme should take into consideration the following factors: (a) the socio-economic situation of the country; (b) the government and state finances; (c) the education policy of the country; (d) the situation and the principal problems of the education system; and (e) the strategy for implementing the nation's educational policy and priorities (or project areas) which stem from that. (IIEP, 1986:16.)

Many international agencies have as one important development objective that technical, economic and other types of support should contribute to equality and rural development. However, whether this is possible or not seems to depend largely on the type of government in the country. Hultin (1986) argues that the following two questions have to be answered before a reform is implemented. First, is the political situation conducive to a reform of the suggested type? And, second, has the country reached the stage of development when the proposed reform could be appropriate?

It is not difficult for an evaluator to find information about a country's political situation, but in general, the evaluator does not study or judge this situation. None the less, it should be taken into consideration in the evaluation study. Also to be considered as part of the programme setting is the socio-economic setting. That is, technical/vocational education projects should be studied in relation not only to the labour-market demands, but also in relation to the overall socio-economic situation. However, it may be difficult to find out whether the skills provided in the technical/vocational programmes correspond to those needed in the society or not, since there are many intervening variables. Besides the factors mentioned here that are to be considered in the programme setting, the cultural patterns and the administrative framework within which a programme operates also need to be reviewed. There are great variances in these factors, among programmes, and these should be accounted for.

4.3 The evaluation setting

When it comes to the evaluation procedure itself, there are some problems in common with other types of educational evaluations, namely those related to paradigms, designs and methodologies. Some such issues will be developed in this section.

As evaluation is more or less a comparative approach, which utilizes scientific concepts and methods, it may vary in, for instance, perspective, scope and domain.

The *perspective* has a number of dimensions, some of which are: (a) holism/atomism; (b) formalism/substantivism; and (c) conflict/consensus. (Alkin and Ellett, 1985; Bacchus, 1988; Bowman, 1988; Lauglo and Lillis, 1988.)

In an atomistic evaluation we focus on the institutions and the skills produced, and we use very formalistic methods to measure the skills. In a holistic approach we may analyse critically what is included - and what is not - in the concept of vocational education as defined by the national authorities. Concerning formalism and substantivism, the evaluation of skills may be used as one example in illustrating the differences in this dimension. If we have a formalistic approach, we are content with the measures that are used in the schools for skills assessment or we use some other tests. In the substantive approach, one can only assume that such tests measure only a part of what really needs to be studied: for example, one must also know what is going on in the occupations which the students are supposed to enter after completing their education. In the latter approach, participant observation in the work-place or interviews with employers might be likely instruments. In relation to the conflict/consensus dimension we may, in principle, refer to some of what has been mentioned in Part One. However, it can be added that projects in relation to socialization and production seldom have a similar meaning to (or identical effects upon) all the people concerned.

By *scope* we mean how large a part of the chain of events, from the initiation and planning via the operation and to the outcomes, is implied in the evaluations. The scope of the evaluation may vary from the national system of vocational education/training down to the introduction and function of a particular "vocational subject" in secondary education, for instance, or down to a particular "vocational school or centre" (Chinapah and Fägerlind, 1986). Thus, the criteria, the indicators, and the methods and techniques to be used for a particular evaluation will vary.

The *domain* may consist of a particular subject in secondary education, a particular school unit, a subsystem, a national system, and so on. Within the large realm of evaluation, we find various levels or aspects that an evaluation could consider. Some which might serve as examples are: (a) a whole system (vocational secondary education, for instance); (b) particular institutions (of certain schools); (c) programmes or projects; (d) particular themes or aspects: curricular, certain subjects, teaching staff, teaching methods, etc.; (e) what are the costs (estimated and analysed in various ways)?; and (f) who gets employment and where? What are his/her personal gains from the vocational training? What are the gains for the employer? For society? Do those with vocational training have higher productivity than those without? And so on.

An evaluation has to place its objects in a social context. When this has been done the following questions are, in general, raised: Who gets in? For how long? Why? With what effects? How does the recruitment take place? Who is selected? What is the principal object for the evaluation? These are only some examples of questions to be raised and answered in an evaluation. (For more detailed lists of issues, variables and indicators, see Grabe, 1983; Hunting et al., 1986; IIEP, 1986). It may be added that the school itself is a variable (or aggregation of variables) that differs considerably in regard to, for instance, the production of various work ethics and the esteem of manual work.

To start from the whole and the macro-level, a project is situated in an environment from which it receives a certain type and amount of input and through which it provides a certain type and amount of output. Bowman (1988:202-3) argues that the surrounding society - and its cultural and technological values - have an influence upon the status of a vocational school, and hence on the recruitment and selection: "The first question to be asked is how supportive society at large is to the values of the course that is to be offered."

Further, it is important to assess and analyse the recruitment and selection of a particular programme. Two reasons which underline the importance of these elements of the environment are: (a) it is important to know which qualities and aspirations the incoming students have since these factors have a certain influence upon the school success and the future careers of the students after completing vocational training; and (b) it is important to assess the equality and equity in access to various types of education.

The project as a system has a number of components (subsystems). In an evaluation it is also necessary to study the input-output between these systems (Soumelis, 1983). What is macro and micro and what is output and input depends on the purpose of the evaluation, and thus, on the definition of the systems and its subsystems that we have made. Some examples will be given in order to demonstrate the idea. If the project to be evaluated is the national system of technical/vocational secondary education in a country, this education is the system and the unit administering this education may be seen as the subsystem. We may find the following subsystems: (a) the decision-making and management subsystem (the Ministry of Education or the body to which the decision-making and executive functions have been delegated); (b) the teacher corps as one subsystem; (c) the curriculum as one subsystem; (d) the logistic subsystem; (e) the selected students as one subsystem; and so on.

If, on the other hand, the project to be evaluated is a particular school, the same subsystems and their relation to each other have to be investigated but only in this particular school. All the subsystems mentioned can be studied in relation to the objectives for this particular school. All these subsystems have to be studied in relation to each other, to the context described in previous sections and to the objectives set for technical/vocational education in general.

The focus is different in the two examples mentioned above. In the latter we might need, and have the resources to make, a more intense and qualitative observation. In the first case we have to collect data on the aspects listed below. Table 5 gives just some examples of what has to be included in a complete and holistic evaluation.

Table 5. Holistic considerations for data collection.

Input	Processes	Output
-number of students enrolled -characteristics of students: socio-economically, geographically, ethnically, etc. -attitudes of students before they start	-curriculum as it is in itself and how it is interpreted and executed in the schools -teaching methods -utilization of buildings, workshops laboratories, etc.	-number of students that graduate from the schools -number of students that fail in the examinations; -skills of graduated students -career of ex-student -productivity of ex-students in comparison to other people employed in the same occupations

The World Bank overview mentioned earlier (Hultin, 1986) demonstrates the following shortcomings in the evaluations that have been made concerning technical/vocational education: (a) no single (evaluation) model can be used everywhere; (b) few studies investigate the internal efficiency of vocational education institutions; and (c) many evaluations have been conducted too soon after the project completion or fail to consider the longer-term impacts.

If the purpose of the study is purely evaluative, the project has to "mature" before it is time for evaluation. For evaluations of technical/vocational education the appropriate time may be more problematic than for other types of educational evaluations, since this type of education is supposed to create competencies or skills which are directly applicable in the society (on the labour market). Whether the skills are relevant or not might be judged according to: (a) the employability of the ex-students (how large a proportion are employed in a relevant sector, in relevant occupations, etc.); and (b) their skills and their productivity in the occupations that they have received.

Unfortunately, (b) cannot be measured until (a) has occurred. Whether (a) occurs or not and how long a time it takes does not necessarily depend on the education given but upon a large number of other factors. In any case, evaluations and other research reports demonstrate that at least a couple of years may pass before ex-students have found suitable occupations. Therefore, technical/vocation education projects are often not mature for evaluation until two years after the first cohort has graduated. If it is a four-year education, a summative type of evaluation cannot take place until six years after the start of the project. Interestingly enough, some studies have dealt with the question of what skills the employers demand or require; yet in general, employers are not able to specify the characteristics they have in mind when hiring new employees. However, this should not prevent the evaluator from trying to find out what the employers think of this matter, especially as this relation with employers may vary greatly from situation to situation.

An overall observation that might be made about the evaluations of technical/vocational education is that there is little interest in internal efficiency (factors that concern the internal affairs of the school system). This, perhaps, is due to the fact that educational researchers have not been greatly involved in the technical/vocational school evaluations thus far.

4.4 Evaluating the programme content

The content of technical/vocational education is very important but often proves difficult to assess as there are so many issues to be dealt with. Yet for many programmes it is this area which deservedly attracts the most attention. Hultin (1986:24) argues - on the basis of a large number of evaluations - that there is "a wide gap between what is happening in the industrial workshop, in the office or on the field and what is done in the school".

The internal aspects of vocational education are roughly the same as those in general education. However, in certain vocational studies some issues are more important to investigate than others. Some examples of these might be: (a) the background and vocational experience of the teachers; (b) the curricula (in relation to the labour-market demands); (c) the contents of specific subjects (in relation to the labour-market demands); (d) the examination system (in relation to the skills that are intended to be produced); (e) the quality of the workshops (in the cases where it is relevant); (f) the effectiveness of management and planning; and (g) the cost-effectiveness of alternative institutions and methods of training (Lillis, 1985; IIEP, 1986).

The content is an internal aspect of the system. It relates to the following: (a) the structure of the system; (b) the curriculum; (c) the teacher quality; (d) the teaching methods and the material framework for teaching/learning; and (e) the examination system. These five elements are explained below.

The structure. There are in general three major structures of vocational education: (a) a parallel system of vocational and academic schools; (b) the diversified secondary schools with pre-vocational and vocational programmes in addition to the academic programmes; and (c) the non-formal training centres (Hultin, 1986). In more detail, the structure concerns the division of the education into forms and levels and the duration of the courses. How long is the course and the school year? Is the duration of the course appropriate in relation to the objectives of the course? Does it correspond to the needs of the agricultural sector, for instance? How is the academic year divided and proportioned - in relation to the seasons of agricultural production, for example?

The curriculum. The definition and operationalization of the curriculum is one of the most problematic points in an evaluation.

The totality of the curriculum is seldom possible to evaluate other than somewhat intuitively or superficially. Instead, certain aspects of the curriculum have to be chosen. The aspects selected depend largely on the purpose of the evaluation. Instead of indicating particular categories or aspects of the curriculum, we shall present some basic questions that should be answered when assessing the curriculum. Is the emphasis placed on the acquisition of a limited number of basic skills and attitudes, or on a general ability to learn skills and attitudes? Which of these is given priority in the objectives? What is needed in the relevant section of the labour market of the country? What is the ratio of the academic, on the one hand, to the practical/vocational, on the other? What is the ratio of academic lessons to practical lessons? Is this ratio compatible with the goals and objectives of the system? Does it correspond to the labour-market needs? Where does the practical part of the education take place: in workshops within the school or in work-places outside the school? What are the relations between the school and the world of work, particularly those sectors that students are preparing for? Is the curriculum relevant to the demands and needs of the labour market? Is it relevant to the pupils - is it essential for them to learn what the school has to offer and the way in which it is offered?

The teacher quality. (Evaluation of the personnel component will be dealt with in Section 4.6. Here we focus mainly on the pedagogical quality of the teachers.) Is the number of competent/qualified teachers sufficient, too high or too low? What are their interests in teaching in the present type of education (in relation to other types)? What is the background of the teachers: purely academic, purely vocational or a mixture? What is their experience in the occupations which they are to teach about?

The teaching methods and material framework for teaching/ learning. Evaluation of teaching methods may be based on one of three distinct types of criteria: (a) the outcomes of the teaching; (b) the learning behaviours or experiences of the pupils that the teaching provides; and (c) the behaviour of the teacher while teaching (Medley, 1985:1735). Any of these criteria may be used in an evaluation. The first is in general used, but in an evaluation of the teaching methods of technical/vocational schools we should have: (a) a broader perspective than that implied in these three criteria; and (b) information about the processes within the schools. A broader perspective includes information about the relations between theory and practice, the relations between experiences in the workshops and the demands of real occupations, and so on.

In an evaluation, it is important to study all the factors that influence the skills and profiles which the students have when they come out of the system. Therefore, we should try to study: (a) the relationships between academic lessons and practical lessons; and (b) the equipment and tools, and their utilization in the workshop on the one hand, and in the work-places to which

the students are supposed to be recruited, on the other hand. The relationship between academic and practical lessons may be of three types, each of which has its own effects upon the students' skills, as well as their attitudes towards the relevant occupations or the relevant sector of the labour market:
1. Mechanical relationship: themes are treated theoretically during the academic lessons and in an order that has not been established on the basis of real work procedures, but rather on the basis of theoretical pedagogy. These themes are rarely followed up in the workshop.
2. Organic relationship: themes treated during the academic lessons are applied during the practical lessons. Problems that appear in practice and require further knowledge are followed up during the academic lessons.
3. There is no relationship whatsoever between the contents of the theoretical and the practical lessons.

In the second case, we can assume that the attitudes of the students towards their future jobs will be more positive and that they will be more motivated, while in the third case, the gap between the academic and the practical/technical/manual is maintained.

The equipment and tools in school workshops are often considerably more advanced and complicated than those existing in work-places outside the school. If so, it is important that the students learn to develop their creativity and ability to "invent new solutions". We should also study how pupils learn and are taught to take their own initiatives and find flexible solutions to problems, particularly if these themes are implied in the goals of the education under evaluation.

The examination system. This is one of the most problematic issues in technical/vocational education and its evaluation. First, there should exist tests or other types of examinations which measure the skills that the education is intended to create. Second, there might be an academic bias in the tests or examinations in that they are loaded towards abilities and skills which are used in an academic context but which are not useful in the world of work. The whole question of relevance may have its focus in the examination system. The type of education that has been implemented and is actually in operation may be very relevant as a whole, and in a macro-perspective, and all other things within the education system may be relevant; but the examination system does not correspond to the rest of the education system, nor to the objectives and/or the needs of the labour market. The questions we are faced with in assessing the examination system are not very easy to answer. For example, does the examination system support the features which are implied in the objectives of education? Does it support or discriminate against abilities and skills that are useful in the labour market? It will demand great creativity on the part of the evaluator if one really wants to examine and understand the effects of the examination system.

4.5 Evaluating logistical components

The facilities, workshops, equipment and tools and teaching materials are, in general, objects of logistical evaluation. In evaluating logistical components, we can first investigate the quantitative aspects. Are there enough buildings, teaching materials, and so on? How are they utilized? Is it possible to decrease the cost per unit (pupil or other unit) through more effective utilization of the resources? Is it possible to improve the quality of the education by increasing the existing resources or by changing the pattern of utilization?

Considering logistics, a large number of possibilities are open if two or more school units co-operate. Sometimes various schools within the same area may utilize the same buildings or the same equipment. Sometimes co-operation between a school and the surrounding industries may decrease the cost (per unit) and/or improve the quality of the education.

The quality and effectiveness of technical/vocational education will be greatly affected by the logistical components involved, especially when compared with other types of preparatory education. The adequacy and utilization of the physical resources (buildings, equipment and materials) can be assessed both quantitatively and qualitatively. Facilities can be measured in unit areas of teaching space or unit costs of equipment. For quantitative measures, there are broad values or norms that are internationally accepted and can serve for comparison.

Qualitatively, we have to find out whether the buildings, furniture, workshops, equipment, and so on, are appropriate to the project objectives and if they are adapted to the local ecological, climatic and socio-cultural conditions. Qualitative assessments can reveal faults and aspects of ineffectiveness that quantitative assessments cannot (Hunting et al., 1986). Here are three examples:
1. Reasonable average utilization of machinery may represent overcrowding for a short amount of time and zero use the rest of the time.
2. While the workshops and equipment may receive ample use, the training exercises and activities guiding the students' utilization may be inappropriate or of poor quality.
3. While the expenditure on equipment may be reasonable, the equipment may be unsuitable for the objectives of the training programme, or unmatched to the occupation areas the training is intended for.

An evaluation of the logistical components has in general to rely on data received through informal interviews with school authorities, teachers, students and others, and more or less intuitive observations from their structured observations of their utilization. It might be necessary to visit some relevant workplaces in order to be able to compare the standard of the school equipment with what exists in the world of work.

4.6 Evaluating personnel components

While much has already been said in previous sections about the teaching staff and other types of personnel, this may not be sufficient. If an evaluation wishes to focus on the personnel component, other considerations must be included.

According to Hultin (1986), schools in developing countries tend to have more difficulties in recruiting and retraining technical/vocational teachers. Many of the teachers thus have little practical experience themselves, as they come fresh from teacher-training courses. Another peculiarity about the personnel component of technical/vocational education concerns the non-teaching personnel. It is not uncommon for these categories of personnel (that do not have pedagogical tasks) to maintain their quantity, even if the number of students and teachers decreases or increases.

In a macro-evaluation we may investigate what types of function are fulfilled by various categories of personnel and their qualifications for these functions. We can also analyse the workload and functions in relation to the number of people employed for each category of functions to be fulfilled in that organization. Such an analysis may show whether there is a balance or not between the workload and the quantity of personnel. In general, it is easier to measure the balance on the educational/pedagogical side than on the administrative side, since the tasks of the teachers are more specified in time than that of other categories of personnel. For a micro evaluation of the personnel component, we will need not only to assess the present state of the staff members, but also to identify deficiencies and training needs. One can do this, in part, via reviews of personnel records and through observation of teaching performance.

An evaluation of the personnel components should consider the procedures for (a) selection; (b) appointment; (c) assignments; and (d) promotion. Besides these procedures, there are several suggested issues and indicators that need to be reviewed in a personnel assessment (Hunting et al., 1986:9). These include both qualitative issues and quantitative indicators:

Qualitative
1. Personnel policy, salaries, and other conditions of service.
2. Selection and qualifications of personnel.
3. Size and quality of personnel, as well as turnover.
4. Size, quality and salaries of support personnel.
5. Personnel development plans and training (pre-service and in-service).

Quantitative
1. Student/teacher ratio (by course or for the programme).
2. Average class size (preferably separated for classroom work and workshop activities).

3. Average teacher workload (normally expressed as teaching hours or contact hours per week).

A school's management and senior staff, while more seldom the subject of evaluation, can be assessed by examining the organizational structure and the management style and effectiveness. This must usually be done qualitatively; however, other key factors in the assessment of an educational programme can serve as supporting data for evaluating management performance.

4.7 Evaluating programme performance

What perhaps most distinguishes evaluations of vocational education from other types of educational evaluation is that the former has as one of its focuses the post-school period, that is, the career of the graduates. Thus, apart from an analysis of the extent to which objectives are realized, other aspects have to be taken into consideration when assessing programme performance, such as:
1. How are the objectives of the particular project to be evaluated in relation to the grand objectives/goals of the national development plans?
2. What are the relations between the various objectives of the project itself? Is there correspondence or contradiction?
3. Are there other structures or units that realize the same objectives (but perhaps at a lower cost)?
4. Does the project attain other goals (desirable or undesirable) other than those it was intended to? Are there so-called hidden goals?

The evaluation criteria, which should be established right from the start of the evaluation (if they are not included in the programme itself), are roughly the same as those utilized in general education. The programme should be: (a) justified with respect to the country's development policy and objectives; (b) effective, that is, produce significant change in the planned direction with a minimum of undesired side-effects, and at a low cost; (c) efficient; (d) relevant; and (e) able to make a contribution to equality (Grabe, 1983; Soumelis, 1983; Chinapah and Fägerlind, 1986; IIEP, 1986). Justification implies that the project corresponds to, or is compatible with, the large-scale goals, whether they be industrialization or land reforms, both of which could make technical and vocational skills necessary.

Efficiency and effectivity relate to the objectives or the goals of the project. The evaluator may judge whether the objectives are good and realistic. Then the task is to find out to what extent the project or programme achieves these, and the extent to which it contributes to other goals as well (good or bad).

Relevance implies that the fulfilment of the goals corresponds to the needs of the society (for instance, that the production of 100 graduates per year from a technical secondary school really is what the country and its labour market need). The relevance (and other criteria as well) may be analysed for the whole programme or project but also for various subsystems and in relation to the society as a whole, to its manpower needs and to the individuals who participate in the project (i.e. the students participating in the education under evaluation).

For an evaluation of equality of access and opportunity, it might be helpful to use a design which considers the following factors (listed in the left-hand column of Table 6) as they pass through the four phases.

Table 6. Factors and indicators to be considered in the evaluation of equality of access and opportunity to technical/vocational education.

	I	II	III	IV
	Recruitment and selection	Pass through the system in the stipulated time	Repeat and/or drop out from the system	Find/don't find employment in relevant sector
1. Sex 2. Socio-economic background 3. Geographical background 4. Ethnic background 5. Results in primary school examinations 6. Attitudes towards the actual type of education		(numbers of students)		

What is the composition according to the background variables of those who are selected and those who are not? Those who pass through the system in stipulated time and those who do not? And what is the rate of employment according to the background variables? If the examination system differentiates between the various factors, the results could also be studied in relation to the background variables. A study of the above-mentioned type would reveal whether or not there is discrimination against students with a certain background (or a combination of background variables). A study of a fishery school in Tunisia showed, for example, that sons of fishermen were heavily underrepresented among the students of the school (due mainly to the selection procedure). Those students who passed through the school did not seek employment as fishermen but were employed as teachers (in general secondary schools or in recently established schools of the same type as the one they had attended), while the sons of fishermen tended to become fishermen within the traditional fishing setting (Daun, 1979).

In evaluating programme performance, it is important to recognize that overall performance depends on various components,

many of which have been reviewed in this chapter. Also, a programme has many inputs and outputs - most of which are measurable - which will need to be considered as a whole when evaluating overall programme performance. On the input side we should consider:
1. The number of graduates as a proportion of students enrolled. We can, for instance, follow one age-group through the system.
2. The time it takes to produce one (or one hundred) graduate(s). For every graduate, how many school years have been spent in the education system (including those who repeat or drop out after some time)?
3. The costs per graduated student. Are the costs higher or lower than in corresponding or similar types of education in the country? What were the costs for the training of others in the relevant occupations who did not have the vocational schooling?
4. The student/teacher ratio. What is it in relation to corresponding or similar types of education? What is it in relation to the objectives of the education?
5. The teaching staff, and the procedures for selection, appointment, assignment and promotion. What are the salaries and other conditions of the teaching staff?
6. Other types of staff. How are they utilized and what is the performance of this personnel, in particular the personnel of the workshops, the libraries, etc.?

On the output side we have the students with their skills, abilities and attitudes. To assess these we have to investigate:
1. The attitudes of the students towards relevant occupations.
2. The cost of producing one student with these skills.
3. The employability of the students.
4. The productivity of the students when they have entered their occupations.

For a broader manpower perspective one needs to know the number of students produced and the number demanded, as well as the qualities produced and the qualities demanded. In addition, one should attempt to find out: (a) the cost-effectiveness of the education and of alternative methods of training; and (b) the output correlation between the training/education system and the employment requirements (Grabe, 1983). In an individual perspective we have to investigate the relation between the individual investments in the actual type of education (economic and other costs) and the salary received in the occupation after completing the education (Soumelis, 1983; Hunting et al., 1986).

An evaluation of a programme's performance should at some point consider cost. Practical subjects within secondary education typically have high capital and recurrent unit costs, and thus are sometimes hard to justify. Not only is technical/vocational education expensive to establish, but it seems more expensive to maintain. As Hultin (1986) points out, there was initially a common belief that the higher cost of technical/vocational education would result in a higher social and private rate of return. This, however, has not been the case.

With respect to costs, there exist a number of sophisticated techniques, but most of them require a rather high quality of data on revenues and expenditures. In a developing country such data are not always available. However, some of the common data and techniques are in general sufficient for estimations of the costs. The scheme in Table 7 shows some of the basic types of data that are necessary. Recurrent and capital expenditures always have to be differentiated and estimated. Within the recurrent costs a distinction should be made between teaching costs and other costs. Capital expenditures (buildings, equipment, etc.) should be estimated per year during a certain period. The duration of this period may be determined by the time that the equipment, for instance, is estimated to function before it has to be replaced. What unit costs should be estimated depends on the purpose of the evaluation. Regardless of the purpose, however, it is in general necessary to estimate the per student costs. Also, if possible, the costs should be compared to those of other comparable schools, subjects, and so on. This is an internal comparison (within the system in question).

Table 7. Basic data for estimating unit cost for technical/ vocational education.

Unit	Recurrent expenditures	Capital expenditures
education system per subject area per school per student etc.		

If it is the purpose, and when data exist, external comparisons should also be made. One example will be given with respect to this. A technical school produces carpenters. In an external comparison we have to find out the costs for the training of carpenters that already work (but without the secondary school course) and compare them with the costs for producing the carpenters from the actual school in question. In a more sophisticated analysis it is also necessary to compare the productivity (or competence) of the secondary school-trained worker with that of the apprenticeship-trained worker.

In the foregoing chapters of Part Two of this book, we have chosen three specific educational areas in which to examine some strategic approaches to educational evaluation. Due to space and other constraints, further areas could not be covered. In Part Three, we shall focus on some practical experiences in evaluating programmes in developing countries related to these three specific areas. We shall draw upon the discussion in the foregoing chapters in order to establish the proper linkages between the theory and practice of educational evaluation.

Part Three

*Experiences in
educational evaluation*

Introduction

This book would be incomplete, or at least deceptive, without a careful presentation and discussion of some practical experiences (successes, limitations and bottlenecks) in the planning, conduct and execution of some educational evaluations. Part Three treats the experiences accrued in the evaluation of three educational programmes and projects in developing countries. The first example is taken from the National Educational Evaluation Study of Primary Education in Mauritius, the second, from the Ethiopian Literacy Campaign Evaluation, and the third, from the Evaluation Study of Industrial Education in Academic Secondary Schools in Kenya. Emphasis will be given to a step-by-step description, presentation and examination of these three educational evaluations.

The overriding aim in Part Three is to provide an overview of these three practical evaluation experiences in the context of developing countries where many of the so-called "theories, paradigms or models of educational evaluation" developed elsewhere become uprooted, non-comprehensive and too far-reaching for their intended application and use. None the less, these three practical experiences have faced this challenge and may contribute significantly to resolving the lacunae in this field. The selection and presentation of these three evaluations are designed so that they both reinforce and complement one another.

Concerning primary education, there are only a few evaluation examples from the developing countries which consider national surveys. There are many reasons for this and one can easily pass the buck to the decision-makers in these countries or to the funding agencies. The National Educational Evaluation Survey in Mauritius (Chapter 5) demonstrates the application and usefulness of survey design. A nationally representative sample of schools and students is chosen. Equality of educational opportunity in primary schooling is evaluated from the standpoints of participation and performance of children differing in age, sex, socio-economic, linguistic and regional backgrounds and attending different types and qualities of schools. Using quantitative evaluation methods, this example will show how different evaluation instruments (questionnaires and tests) and statistical techniques for data management and analysis (SPPS, Partial Least Squares - PLS, and LISREL programmes) can be applied in the field of educational evaluation.

Due to constraints of space, Chapter 5 avoids treating the findings from the study. Instead, emphasis is placed on the practical experiences in the planning and conduct of this evaluation. The nature and content of the evaluation are presented and discussed. The discussion includes the theoretical framework, the methodological approach, the evaluation instruments and data base, the procedures in data collection and data processing, and the structure of analysis. This evaluation highlights the importance of training field assistants for the administration of the evaluation instruments (questionnaires and tests). It also indicates how important it is for educational evaluation in developing countries to ensure pilot-testing before finalizing instruments, data-collection procedures and analyses. Pilot studies can significantly contribute to all phases of an educational evaluation; this is revealed clearly in the case of the Ethiopian Literacy Campaign Evaluation (ELCE) in Chapter 6.

The experience from the ELCE is a far-reaching example of a large-scale evaluation in the context of a developing country. It reveals how difficult it is to plan and execute a massive evaluation undertaking in the absence of adequate qualified evaluation personnel. This project illuminates certain practical issues in planning and implementing educational evaluations in the context of a developing country, namely, the need for: (a) better linkages between all phases of educational evaluations; (b) pilot study or pre-testing; and (c) staff development in educational evaluation and research. We shall observe the progress along these lines when examining the achievements made in Phase II of the evaluation. This evaluation experience also shows how on-the-spot tailored training can strengthen the capacity for educational evaluation.

The evaluation consists of three phases but only the first two completed phases are presented and discussed in Chapter 6. Phase I deals with the evaluation of the literacy campaign in urban areas while Phase II deals with the evaluation in rural areas. The third phase, not considered in this chapter, is the evaluation of the post-literacy phase of the campaign. In the evaluation of Phases I and II, a combination of quantitative and qualitative methods of evaluation is utilized (questionnaires, interviews, observation schedules, checklists, field notes, etc.). This strategy proved to be a difficult one in Phase I but after the experience gained in that phase, it was possible to limit its scope and streamline procedures for Phase II. This evaluation had the mandate to analyse the process (i.e. all activities involved in the implementation of the literacy campaign), to analyse the impact of the campaign and to analyse the literacy data collected. Data were collected from various types of instruments and from a variety of informants (adult educational officers, adult teachers, adult literates). The evaluation of literacy skills was assessed through tests in: (a) reading comprehension; (b) ability to express ideas in writing; and (c) arithmetic. Some details are given in this chapter as to how the data were collected, processed, analysed and reported. In all respects, the practical experiences from Phase I were genuinely studied in order to ensure a better quality of evaluation in Phase II.

Finally, in Chapter 7, the practical experiences from the Evaluation Study of Industrial Education in Academic Secondary Schools in Kenya are summarized. To complement the other two experiences, this one has both cross-sectional and longitudinal designs (e.g. tracer studies) and applies both quantitative and

Introduction

qualitative evaluation methods and techniques. This is a difficult educational programme area to be evaluated, yet this endeavour penetrates questions of great significance to educational evaluation in general. Although the focus is on industrial education, many of the organizational, conceptual, methodological and analytical issues in this evaluation have direct relevance to other educational evaluation programmes and projects.

The role and function of technical/vocational education in Kenya are examined first in Chapter 7. Then emphasis is given to the Kenya-Sweden Technical and Industrial Education Project (KS) which has been evaluated. The evaluation consists of nine major steps: (1) documentary analysis of the aims and objectives of the Industrial Education (IE) Programme; (2) the analysis of educational policy in Kenya and the aspects of direct relevance for the IE evaluation study; (3) review of international literature; (4) surveys of students; (5) tracer studies; (6) examination results analysis; (7) survey of employers; (8) cost analysis; and (9) documentary analysis of the syllabuses of IE and its relationship to other post-primary practical or vocational education. The practical experiences from this evaluation endeavour are examined in light of the practices and principles for evaluating technical/vocational education presented and discussed in Chapter 4. A number of evaluation questions related to programme content, logistical and personnel components and project performance are considered in this chapter in order to reflect the type and quality of information required for evaluating technical/vocational educational programmes and projects.

5. The National Educational Evaluation Study of Primary Education in Mauritius

5.1 Basic evaluation questions at the primary education level

A number of questions that were important for policy decision-making and relevant to the commitment to greater equality of educational opportunity were considered in the evaluation. Some of these are listed below.

Are primary schools in Mauritius divisive along social, cultural and economic lines? In other words, do certain school sectors (government rural, government urban, aided rural and aided urban) contain more children from certain specific socio-economic, ethnic or cultural groups?

Do school inputs (physical facilities, services, teacher-body, etc.) differ within and between the school sectors?

What sex differences are there in respective school sectors?

Do younger children perform better than older ones in the Certificate of Primary Education (CPE) examination?

Do children from different socio-economic and ethnic backgrounds perform differently in different school sectors?

Are there sizable inter- and intra-regional differences in scholastic performance?

Are there differences in the scholastic performance of children attending the government and aided school sectors and in different regions (rural as contrasted with urban)?

Can certain specific types of home influence on the children's scholastic performance be identified in the four school sectors?

Are certain specific types of school influence on the children's scholastic performance found in the four school sectors?

What is the relative importance of the home and school for determining how well children will perform scholastically in these sectors?

How do the effects of the home and school factors on the scholastic performance of children differ from school sector to school sector?

Do the interrelationships between home and school factors, and the way they operate to influence the scholastic performance of children, differ from school sector to school sector?

Do differences between school sectors reinforce inequalities in performance among primary school children?

Answers to such questions as these were based on an analysis of data collected from a nationally representative sample of primary schools and pupils in the last grade of primary education.

In this section, we shall also briefly outline the aims and objectives of the evaluation, especially as these relate to the questions above. The overall aim of this study was to examine the extent to which policies aimed towards equality of educational opportunity were put into effect at the primary education level in Mauritius. The right to attend primary educational institutions was examined in terms of children's participation and performance in primary schools.

The specific objectives of the study were:
1. To describe the home and school environments of learning.
2. To identify major similarities and differences in these environments.
3. To study the differences between pupils, their school participation and their scholastic performance in four distinct school sectors: (i) government rural; (ii) government urban; (iii) aided rural; and (iv) aided urban.
4. To examine the importance of specific home and school factors in determining variations in scholastic performance in each of the four school sectors separately.
5. To assess the relative importance of the home and school predictors on scholastic performance in each of the four sectors separately.
6. To compare across the four school sectors the types of interrelationships between the home and school factors and the way they interact to determine scholastic performance.

5.2 The national setting of the evaluation study

The development of popular or mass education in Mauritius is of rather recent date. Until the 1950s, which marked the beginning of majority rule, educational development under both French and British colonial administrations was strongly influenced by segregationist and separationist policies. These policies aimed not only at maintaining a "have/have not" split in colonial Mauritius but also at reinforcing racial, colour, ethnic, religious, linguistic and regional inequalities between the settler populations. The majority groups among the settler populations were then, and had long been, dominated by a small minority group, i.e. the French sugar oligarchy--the French settler group and their descendants, the Franco-Mauritians.

The march towards majority rule went under the political slogan "Education for All". Education of the masses was conceived as being a political instrument for greater social, cultural, economic and political equality in the former colonial society. Educational development after political independence from Britain in 1968 was characterized by a trade-off between policies aimed at achieving greater equality of educational opportunity and policies aimed at developing human resources. The former set of policies was geared towards meeting the fast-changing social, cultural and political needs of Mauritian society and the latter towards satisfying the fast-changing manpower needs of the Mauritian economy. This trade-off had to a large extent influenced the deployment and use of the country's available educational resources and created an imbalance between quantitative growth and the qualitative improvement of the education system. Universal free primary education, although not compulsory, was achieved in the early 1970s and since 1977 education has been free at all levels.

The evaluation study was principally interested in examining policies which aimed at bringing about greater equality of educational opportunity in Mauritius. These policies still constitute the core of the Mauritian Government's educational development strategy. In the First Plan for social and economic development (1971-75) the commitment to an overall policy of educational equality was expressed in the following three educational objectives: (a) free education for all children at the primary level; (b) opportunity for secondary and vocational training for at least 60 per cent of the boys in the age-group 15-19 by 1980; and (c) equality of educational opportunity for all according to their educational potential.

The democratization of the Mauritius education system and the even distribution of schools and colleges over the country, so as to achieve a balance between educational facilities in urban and rural areas, were the major educational objectives of the Second Plan (1975-80). The Third Plan, under the same regime (1980-82), emphasized the importance of improving the existing educational infrastructure and of ensuring its more even distribution between rural and urban areas.

The change of government after the election of June 1982 was characterized by a further movement to achieve overall equality in Mauritian society. In the new government programme, greater equality in educational opportunity was emphasized through, among other measures, the reintroduction of free university education (abolished in 1979), the establishment of comprehensive or basic education up to Standard III of the secondary school level and the elimination of educational inequalities emanating from the cultural or linguistic backgrounds of children, i.e. by raising the status of the Oriental languages, namely the widely spoken Bhojpuri and the lingua franca, Patois Creole. These two languages (although Patois Creole is still a dialect) would therefore occupy a stronger place in curriculum development and in examination reforms. At that time, the primary education curriculum and the examination system at this level were totally dependent on the teaching and learning of the two foreign languages, English and French.

As in most countries, policies, plans and targets for educational development in Mauritius tended to be very ambitious in nature and their implementation determined by both internal and external conditions. More recently, the government decided to close down some secondary schools, leaving 250 secondary school teachers out of work, a decision imposed as a result of external economic pressures.

5.3 Why primary education?

The emphasis in the evaluation was whether and how children at the primary education level in Mauritius were given equal treatment in schools and an equal chance to exercise their right to education. Over the years, inequalities in performance among children completing primary school (Standard VI) had been an alarming problem. Over half of the examinees at the end of primary schooling were not qualifying for further education after having been advanced from one grade to another through the automatic promotion system which prevailed in primary schools.

The examination at the end of primary schooling was officially designed for certification and for selection to the different secondary school institutions in the country. These primary and secondary institutions varied markedly. Over one-third of the pupils in the last grade of the primary education cycle (Standard VI) repeated that grade two or more times. Children were allowed to remain in primary school until they were 12 years old. In 1978, community schools, now called pre-vocational schools, were created for those children who would otherwise drop out from the school system for ever. Additionally, in 1980, a new examination, the Certificate of Primary Education (CPE), was introduced at the end of the primary education cycle in order to reduce the selective and competitive nature of the two previous examinations, the Primary School Leaving Certificate (PSLC) and the Junior Scholarship Examination (JSE). The JSE had been fervently criticized before this, mainly because it forced children into a frantic competition and compelled parents to pay for private tuition in order that their children might succeed in this examination which was used to select, out of a school population of approximately 35,000 pupils, some top 400 "high achievers" who would be admitted to the best government or government-supported secondary school institutions in the country.

Most Mauritian scholars viewed the introduction of the CPE, or the reform of the examination system, as a weak solution to the alarming problem of educational inequality. Research examining other sources of inequality in children's performance has recently begun. Some of these additional sources of inequality were investigated in the evaluation study through a national survey of school participation and determinants of scholastic performance.

5.4 Theoretical framework

The theoretical framework for the evaluation was largely guided and formed by an extensive literature review. This framework was then used for developing a conceptual model of school learning. The literature review had shown that research dealing with children's school participation and scholastic performance was influenced by diverse theoretical, methodological and empirical developments. Thus, in this section, we shall review the development of the theoretical framework by highlighting relevant parts of the reviewed literature.

Educational research is an interdisciplinary area of inquiry drawing upon the work of psychologists, sociologists, economists, anthropologists, social-psychologists, methodologists and many others. Karabel and Halsey (1977) have classified the outstanding trends, theories and preoccupations of educational research as follows:
1. Functionalist theories of education.
2. The economic theory of human capital.
3. Methodological empiricism (within which special importance is attached to empirical studies of educational equality).
4. Conflict theories of education.
5. The intellectual tradition in educational research and the challenge of the "new sociology of education".

Over the years, equality of educational opportunity has been at the centre of the educational research which assessed the role of education in the process of social stratification and/or social change in given societal settings. Two rival camps eventually arose, with the functionalists on one side and the conflict theorists on the other. Karabel and Halsey (1977) have argued that the functionalists often saw the education system as offering opportunity for the mobility of individuals, while the conflict theorists found that education helped maintain a system of structural inequality. Similar arguments were raised during the course of the intense heredity-environment controversy (see Husén, 1974).

The multiple environmental influences on school learning have been the principal concern of social-psychologists for some years now. It is imperative today in understanding the factors or forces impinging on children's performance in school, especially in a situation where education is a driving force for greater social, cultural, economic, regional and political equality. The environmental social-psychological approach provided a comprehensive theoretical framework for an understanding of the multiple environmental influences on school learning. The importance of this approach has long been recognized.

Although the environmental social-psychological approach had been refined considerably over the years, much of its impetus was still drawn from the classical work of Bloom (1964), *Stability and Change in Human Characteristics*. One of the main conclusions from this work was that:

> Put briefly, the increased ability to predict long-term consequences of environmental forces and developmental characteristics places new responsibilities on the home, the school, and the society. If these responsibilities are not adequately met, society will suffer in the long run. If these responsibilities are neglected, the individual will suffer a life of continual frustration and alienation. The responsibilities are great, the tasks ahead are difficult, and only through increased understanding of the interrelations between environments and individual development will we be able to secure more adequate solutions. (Bloom, 1964:231.)

The environmental social-psychological approach has often been used to develop conceptual models of school learning. Two models of this kind were studied in the literature review, the Marjoribanks model (1974) for home environments of learning and the Harnishfeger and Wiley model (1976) for school or classroom environments of learning. The virtue of these two models was that the environments of school learning were defined both in terms of global environmental indicators and characteristics, e.g. social status, family size, curriculum-institutional factors, teacher background and pupil background, and in terms of social-psychological or process variables, e.g. achievement press, academic guidance, intellectuality in the home, the pupil's educational activities and their relations to those of the teacher. In other words, process variables referred to what went on between parents and children at home and between teachers and pupils at school within the context of school learning.

5.5 Methodological approach

On the basis of the review of literature, a conceptual model of school learning was then developed for the evaluation study and is shown in Figure 5. Both the home and school environments of learning were considered in this investigation, and the distinction between global characteristics and process variables was retained. There was also an interest in studying the way the home and school environments interacted to influence performance.

The conceptual model of school learning fulfilled various functions in the study; among other purposes it was used for the development and construction of relevant instruments, i.e. questionnaires and cognitive tests, and for planning different types of analysis, i.e. from univariate to multivariate analyses.

There were five blocks of variables in the conceptual model of school learning. These blocks referred to: (1) <u>Home and Pupils' Characteristics</u>; (2) <u>Home Processes</u>; (3) <u>School Characteristics</u>; (4) <u>School Processes</u>; and (5) <u>Pupils' Scholastic Performance</u>. A pathway influence among these blocks was indicated by one-way arrows and captured the general hypothesized causal relationships between them. Some variables or related concepts were presented for each of these five blocks. The first block of variables, Home and Pupils' Characteristics, consisted of exogenous variables and was assumed to be influenced by any of them. The remaining four blocks had endogenous or dependent variables. They were assumed to be influenced by at least one of the blocks of variables in the model:

ENVIRONMENTAL CHARACTERISTICS

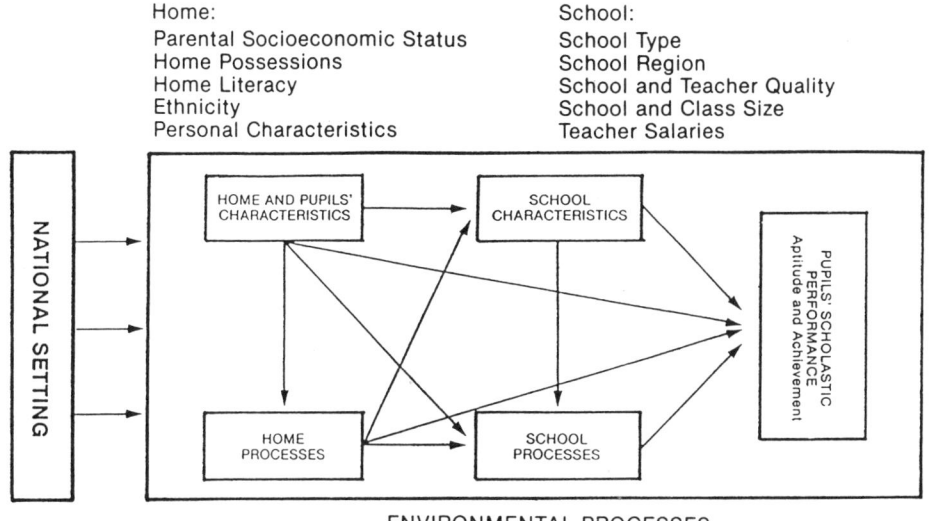

Home:
Parental Socioeconomic Status
Home Possessions
Home Literacy
Ethnicity
Personal Characteristics

School:
School Type
School Region
School and Teacher Quality
School and Class Size
Teacher Salaries

ENVIRONMENTAL PROCESSES

Home:
Parental Educational Support
Access and Provision of Private Tuition
Economic Support to School Needs

School:
Teaching-Learning Processes
Teacher Behavior
Pupil's Classroom Activities
Pupil-Teacher Interaction

Fig. 5. A conceptual model of school learning. After Chinapah (1983a:53).

The verbal interpretation of the causal relationships between the five blocks of variables was summarized in the sixteen general hypotheses listed below:

Influences on home processes
1. Home characteristics have direct positive effects on home processes.

Influences on school characteristics
2. Home characteristics have positive effects on school characteristics.

3. Home processes have direct positive effects on school characteristics.
4. There are indirect effects of home characteristics on school characteristics as mediated by home processes.

Influences on school processes
5. Home characteristics have direct positive effects on school processes.
6. Home processes have direct positive effects on school processes.
7. School characteristics have direct positive effects on school processes.
8. The effects of home characteristics on school processes are indirect as mediated by home processes and school characteristics.
9. The effects of home processes on school processes differ according to different school characteristics.

Influences on pupil's scholastic performance
10. Home characteristics have direct positive effects on pupils' scholastic performance.
11. Home processes have direct positive effects on pupils' scholastic performance.
12. School characteristics have direct positive effects on pupils' scholastic performance.
13. School processes have direct positive effects on pupils' scholastic performance.
14. There are indirect effects of home characteristics on pupils' scholastic performance via home processes, school characteristics and school processes.
15. The effects of home processes on pupils' scholastic performance are indirect as mediated by school characteristics and school processes.
16. The effects of school characteristics on pupils' scholastic performance differ according to different types of school processes.

Before presenting the sampling design and data-collection procedures that were used in the evaluation, the following points should be considered. First, the sixteen general hypotheses were examined in a later part of the study where multivariate analyses of determinants of children's scholastic performance within and between the four school sectors were conducted. In testing these general hypotheses, the blocks were operationalized in terms of latent variables or constructs based on a number of indicators. It was imperative in the study to examine whether, and the extent to which, the scholastic performance of pupils differed from school sector to school sector. Therefore multivariate analysis was carried out separately in each sector and simultaneously across the four sectors. Second, before turning to the multivariate analysis of determinants of scholastic performance within and between school sectors, a general description of the home and school environments of learning was presented. Third, this description was then followed by a study of the association (non-causal relationship) between differences among pupils (age, sex, ethnic and socio-economic) and their participation and scholastic performance in the four school sectors.

Sampling procedures

The target population in this study consisted of pupils in the final grade of primary education (Standard VI) in Mauritius. At the end of the primary education cycle, these pupils have to take a national examination which is aimed at certification and selection for further institutions in the country. As mentioned earlier, a new examination, the CPE, was set up in 1980 with the overriding aim of reducing the selective and competitive bias of the two former examinations. The target population was in this evaluation the first group of pupils taking the new CPE 1980 examination.

A list of 268 schools (including a few secondary schools) with some 31,398 CPE candidates was made available in February 1980 for sampling purposes. The following information was also available about the target population of schools: (a) size of school; (b) type of school - government or aided; and (c) school district - rural or urban. Roughly 5 per cent of the 1980 CPE candidates were sampled. The sample size corresponded to a standard error equal to 8 per cent of a standard deviation of the mean and an intra-class correlation of 0.3. This meant roughly a sample size of 1,500 CPE candidates. However, during that same period, Mauritius was visited by severe cyclones and some primary schools were used as centres for refugees. Instead of 1,500 CPE candidates, the original sample size was increased to 1,650, i.e. by 10 per cent. This 10 per cent increase took into account losses due to absenteeism, dropouts or transfers of CPE candidates from one school to another, and it eventually accounted for losses due to the effects of the cyclones.

A stratified two-stage probability sample of schools and pupils was drawn. In the first stage, schools were selected randomly from different strata: (a) size - small, medium and big; (b) type - government and aided (in the latter a few private secondary schools presenting CPE candidates were also included); and (c) region - rural and urban. The second stage consisted of a simple random sampling of pupils within the selected schools. Since streaming pupils by ability (low ability, average ability, high ability) was practised at the CPE grade as well as in the other grades of primary education in Mauritius, it was necessary to have data from pupils belonging to different streams. In each selected school some 25-35 pupils were randomly chosen from the different CPE streams or sections. The product of the two sampling fractions (i.e. that of schools, and that of pupils within selected schools) was held constant. Large schools had more chance of being selected than small schools, but this was counterbalanced by their being represented in the sample by a smaller proportion of their population of pupils, and each member of the target population had a non-zero chance of selection in the total sample (Peaker, 1975).

Altogether, a nationally representative sample of 54 schools with 1,650 CPE candidates was drawn. All of the selected 54 schools participated in the study and the achieved sample of pupils was very close to the sample size expected, i.e. 1,456 as compared to 1,500. In the distribution of schools and pupils by stratum, only one stratum, the small aided urban school, was empty and had no CPE candidates represented in the sample. This was due to its negligible representation in the target population of schools and pupils.

5.6 Evaluation instruments and data base

Data on the five blocks of variables in the conceptual model of school learning were collected from four sets of questionnaires and from several sets of cognitive instruments. The original sets of questionnaires and aptitude tests together with the manuals prepared for the Field Research Assistants (FRAs) for the fieldwork and coding exercise can be seen in Chinapah (1983b). Below, we shall briefly summarize and comment on the questionnaires and the cognitive instruments utilized, as well as put into perspective the data base involved.

Pupil questionnaire (PQ). The pupil questionnaire consisted of 119 items. It referred mainly to the pupil's personal characteristics and academic-related needs, workload, attitudes and opinions towards schooling, peer-group characteristics, and educational and occupational expectations.

Family household questionnaire (FQ). The family household questionnaire was principally designed to gather information about the pupils' home environments of learning and was answered by parents. Usually such types of data are collected directly from the pupils themselves, but the pupils involved in the study were too young (10-13 years of age) to recall, for example, the number of years their father and mother had attended school, or to know the monthly income of their family or the linguistic background of their parents. It is also important to remember that certain information on the home environments of learning had to be collected from the pupils' family directly, e.g. information on parental attitudes towards schooling, reasons for the choice of a given school, the degree to which parents were concerned with and participated in their children's school activities and their educational and occupational expectations for their children. The family household questionnaire consisted of a total of 134 items measuring the home environment of learning both in terms of home characteristics and home process variables.

School questionnaire (SQ). The school questionnaire was the longest one in the study and contained 165 items. In it, the school head-teachers were asked to provide information on their school. Data were collected from them on school and class size, school physical facilities, school services, teacher salaries, facilities in the school neighbourhood, curricula and extra-curricula facilities and instructional time. In addition, information was collected on the head-teachers' personal characteristics, qualifications and experience, their assessment of the facilities and services available at the school, how often school inspectors visited the school and the purpose of such visits, and the role of the Parent-Teacher Association in the school.

Teacher questionnaire (TQ). Unlike the school questionnaire, which presented data from the school environments of learning as a whole, the teacher questionnaire was designed to depict the classroom learning environments of the CPE candidates. In Mauritius, the primary school pupils are assigned to one teacher, their class teacher. The number of teachers for a particular grade corresponds to the number of classes or sections for that grade in given schools. Children taking an Oriental language (which is optional in the primary school curriculum) also have access to an Oriental-language teacher; however, Oriental-language teachers were not included in the study.

The teacher questionnaire was addressed to the CPE class teacher and contained a total of 82 items. Information on the CPE class teacher included facts about personal characteristics, academic qualifications, training and experience, the size of the class, the sex distribution of pupils in the class, how the pupils were streamed in the class (ability group), the teacher's attitudes towards streaming and automatic promotion, the frequency with which different methods of teaching and assessment were used, the teacher's attitudes towards the existing school facilities and school services, and so on.

The response rate was generally high for these four categories of participants, i.e. pupils, parents, school head-teachers and teachers. As is always the case, not all items in the questionnaires were answered by the respondents. Of the 1,456 family household questionnaires (corresponding to the size of the achieved sample of CPE candidates) 1,286 or 88.3 per cent were filled out and returned by parents. Although the pupils in all 54 selected schools participated in the study, data from the school questionnaires for four schools were not supplied. In these 54 schools there were 215 CPE sections with the same number of CPE class teachers. A very high response rate was achieved for the teacher questionnaire (97.7 per cent), representing data collected from the 210 CPE class teachers. It should be mentioned that a massive amount of data was collected for this study and data-reduction exercises were important for the various types of analysis intended, e.g. variables with greater than 25 per cent missing cases were dropped at the very early stage of the analysis (Peaker, 1975; Heyneman and Loxley, 1982).

Cognitive Instruments. Pupils' scholastic performance, the fifth block in the conceptual model, was measured by two categories of cognitive instruments. The first was a measure of the general aptitude of pupils and comprised selected items from the standardized tests used in the International Association for the Evaluation of Educational Achievement (IEA) cross-national survey (see Thorndike, 1973; Lewis and Massad, 1975; Peaker, 1975; Walker, 1976). The second was a measure of the academic achievement of pupils and was based on tests in four core subjects of the CPE national examination. Aptitude was measured by the total scores of pupils on 80 items from the original IEA tests in: (a) Word Knowledge for Population I; (b) English as a Foreign Language for Population II; and (c) Reading Comprehension for Population I and II. After the analysis of the results from the pilot testing, only a few items from the tests in English as a Foreign Language (22 items) and Reading Comprehension (18 items) were retained. All 40 items on the Word Knowledge test were kept. The reliability (alpha coefficient) for the 80 items measuring aptitude was 0.835. A coefficient of this size is reasonably high (Cronbach, 1951; Nunally, 1967; Bohrnstedt, 1969). Pupils taking the aptitude tests were informed that these tests had nothing to do with certification or selection purposes and had been originally designed for cross-national studies. The FRAs administered the three IEA sub-tests and gave the pupil questionnaire on the same day at each selected school. The administration of the pupil questionnaire and the IEA sub-tests lasted roughly two hours.

Achievement data on the sample taking the CPE examination at the end of the school year (1980) consisted of the total scores that these pupils had in the four CPE subjects: English, French, mathematics and geography. The highest mark that a CPE candidate can obtain in one of these subjects was 100. The marks from all these four subjects constituted a global measure of the CPE candidate's achievement. As mentioned before, the CPE examination was intended to reduce the selective and competitive bias of previous examinations at this grade. Data on the CPE examination were available for most of the pupils in the sample (1,367 pupils or 93.8 per cent).

5.7 Data Collection and data processing

The Ministry of Education and Cultural Affairs (MECA) and the Mauritius Institute of Education (MIE) were of great assistance in the organization and administration of data collection. A national co-ordinator was appointed from the MIE to serve during the entire period when the field-work was going on. The period lasted for two months (May-June 1980). Earlier, however, three schools were chosen for the pilot-testing of the instruments which took place in September and October 1979.

The pilot-testing exercise was organized and intended to serve several purposes. First, during the period of pilot-testing, discussions were held with the MECA and MIE concerning the preparation for the field-work, i.e. resources required (financial support, transportation and personnel) and administrative procedures (e.g. contacts with educational officers and representatives of the Government Teachers' Union, GTU). Second, discussions were held at the MIE about the selection and training of FRAs for the administration of questionnaires and tests during the field-work. Third, the possibilities for data transformation onto magnetic tapes in Mauritius were explored. The firm of Blanche Birger and Company agreed to serve the study in this capacity. Fourth, the administration of the instruments in the three pilot schools was carefully studied. It was found that, for reasons of language, pupils had great difficulty completing their questionnaires and understanding the instructions for the cognitive tests since these instruments were in English.

It was decided that, for purposes of the field-work, the FRAs would translate these instruments into Patois Creole, the lingua franca of almost every pupil. Finally, the experiences from pilot-testing were used to improve the instruments (phrasing of questions, and formats of the questionnaires and tests) and to maintain a reasonable degree of validity and reliability for the field-work.

Some thirty FRAs were recruited among Teacher's Diploma students of the MIE for the field-work. The FRAs participated in a series of seminars dealing with administration of the questionnaires and tests. A manual was also prepared for them. The selected 54 schools were visited twice by the FRAs. During the first visit, school head-teachers and CPE teachers were informed about the nature of the investigation and the methods of data collection. The school questionnaire (SQ), the teacher questionnaire (TQ) and the family household questionnaire (FQ) were also distributed during the first visit. During the second visit, the three sets of questionnaires, SQ, TQ and FQ, were collected on the same day as the pupil questionnaire (PQ) and the aptitude tests (IEA sub-tests) were administered. The second visit took place two weeks after the first visit. In most cases two FRAs were assigned to a single school, and none covered more than two schools on the same day.

Although data from the CPE examinations were delayed for eleven months after the original data collection from the field-work, separate files and code-books were prepared in advance for each set of instruments. In some analyses, it was more convenient to treat the data from each file separately, e.g. for the description of the home and school environments of learning. In bivariate and multivariate analyses, all the data were merged into one file. The data processing was time-consuming because it was necessary to identify wild codes, to eliminate variables with more than 25 per cent missing cases, and so on. The data analysis took place in Stockholm, at the Institute of International Education.

5.8 Structure of analysis

Simple analytical techniques were used for the descriptive parts of the study, e.g. univariates and bivariates. Here the home and school environments of learning were described in terms of both structural and process variables. Determinants of pupils' scholastic performance were examined with more complex analytical tools, i.e. from the conventional Educational Production Function (EPF) analysis and commonality analysis to sophisticated path analysis with latent variables using the Partial Least Squares (PLS) method and a statistical comparative method based on LISREL analysis. Each of these analytical tools had a given function in this evaluation study. For example, the EPF analysis and the commonality analysis were used to compare the results of this study with those of other studies using similar analytical tools. The PLS method was used to account for determinants of scholastic performance (direct, indirect and total effects) from a within-school-sector perspective while the LISREL method was used to account for determinants of scholastic performance across the four school sectors based on simultaneous path analyses.

A pervasive problem in such an evaluation endeavour was the absence of opportunities to compare the empirical evidence in the study with evidence obtained from similar investigations carried out in Mauritius. At the time of the study, no national survey of the scholastic performance of primary school children had been performed, despite the alarming problem of unequal performance at the primary level. Many of the inputs therefore had to be drawn primarily from research and evaluation studies carried out elsewhere, even though the particular Mauritian situational context was respected (e.g. in the construction of reliable instruments for assessing the home and school environments of learning of the Mauritian child).

Although a nationally representative sample of schools and pupils was used, the study only included pupils from the last grade of the primary education cycle: the CPE candidates. Evaluation and research that follow the performance of primary school pupils from one grade to another, and that also follow the CPE candidates after the primary education cycle, would have contributed greatly to an understanding of the equality of educational opportunity issues in the country and served basically as a guide for educational policy decision-making in Mauritius.

The theoretical, methodological and analytical approach used in this evaluation permitted a critical examination of specific policy questions about primary education in Mauritius. In the absence of such an approach, within-school-sector mechanisms would have been hidden and important dimensions of educational inequality would not have been accounted for.

In some countries, a great amount of resources (personnel, financial, technical and material) are required to conduct national evaluations of certain educational programmes. In Chapter 6, we shall draw upon the experience from the Ethiopian Literacy Campaign Evaluation (ELCE) to examine the extent to which personnel, financial, technical and material resources may or may not determine the quality of such a large evaluation study. The ELCE consisted of three phases. The experience from the two first phases will be presented and discussed. It will also be possible to see how the experience from the evaluation undertaken during the first phase was used to improve the quality of the evaluation carried out in the second phase of the study.

6. *The Ethiopian Literacy Campaign Evaluation*

6.1 Background to the Ethiopian Literacy Campaign

In years past, Ethiopia, an African nation with a population of 42 million, had one of the lowest rates of literacy in the world. In part, this stifled the economic, social and political development of this largely subsistence agricultural nation.

The socialist revolution of February 1974 brought about extensive change in Ethiopia. It was within the context of this change that the National Literacy Campaign came into being. The programme of the National Democratic Revolution issued far-reaching goals for Ethiopian education in 1976. These goals considered education to be a vital instrument in the development of production, scientific inquiry and socialist consciousness. After all, one of Ethiopia's greatest available resources is her people. The general government objectives in the development of human resources included: (a) the eradication of illiteracy; (b) the improvement of the quality of general education and training; and (c) the production of high-level manpower in both quantity and quality. This literacy objective, which interests us most here, figured in the overall policy of the government as universal literacy was one of the first steps highlighted in the Ten Year Perspective Plan.

In July 1979 a National Literacy Campaign was initiated. It was felt that literacy was a right which should be guaranteed to all citizens, and further, literacy was considered as a key element in the country's development. One of the overall goals of the campaign was to provide literacy for all citizens between the ages of 8 and 49. The campaign has been an ongoing programme that has continued for over a decade now. The literacy rate at the onset of the campaign was estimated to be 7 per cent, while by 1986 the it had climbed to 62.4 per cent (Makonnen, 1987). Considering the conditions and environment in which the campaign was carried out, this is a remarkable achievement.

The original objectives for Phase I of the National Literacy Campaign were: (a) the eradication of illiteracy from socialist Ethiopia by 1987; (b) the use of literacy skills to acquire knowledge which can be used in the promotion of economic, social, cultural and political development; (c) the laying of a foundation for continuing and lifelong education; and (d) the creation of a socialist culture in Ethiopia.

The campaign's administrative structure was set up parallel with the national administrative structure, in the 15 administrative regions that it covered. Addis Ababa, the capital, was also considered as an administrative region. Each region in Ethiopia is divided into provinces, known as "Awrajas", of which there are 106.

The Awrajas are divided into 604 districts or "Weredas". Below the Weredas, there are basic administrative units in urban and rural areas of the country. In the rural areas they are known as "Yegebevoch Mahiber," or peasant associations, of which there are nearly 20,000; in the urban areas they are referred to as "Yekebele Mahiber", or urban dweller associations. This has been the predominant administrative structure since the Ethiopian popular revolution of 1974. At each administrative level, right down to the urban dweller associations and the peasant associations, a Literacy Campaign Co-ordinating and Executive Committee (LCCEC) was established. Under each LCCEC, there were four subcommittees that had the responsibility of planning, implementing and evaluating the literacy campaign.

Each literacy centre was run by a centre representative who organized the literacy project, the placement of adults and teachers, and the distribution of materials. In addition to this, it was the responsibility of the centre representative to take care of data collection, compilation and upkeep while overseeing the daily activities of the centre. Depending on the enrolment and the availability of qualified teachers, a literacy centre could have between eight and ten literacy teachers in a given round.

The campaign was organized in two rounds conducted every twelve months. During the first round all those illiterate between the ages of 8 and 49 in the community were invited to attend classes. The second round was for those who had been unable to attend the previous round or who had failed in the examination and required remedial tutoring. These rounds were referred to as the "attack" and "mop-up" rounds respectively. During the mop-up round, post-literacy activities were also organized for those who had been successful and gained their certificates. Each of the campaign rounds was intended to last about four months. It usually took participants three or four rounds before they achieved their certificate.

Upon enrolment, the adults were placed in one of the following three class levels according to their abilities: (a) beginners' class; (b) remedial class; or (c) post-literacy class. In addition to the post-literacy classes, reading rooms were set up in most of the literacy centres to reinforce the skills developed in the first two class levels. The class hours were usually arranged according to the needs and preferences of the majority of the class participants, and were organized in three-hour shifts, arranged at different times to accommodate the participants. However, classroom observations later showed that nearly half of the centres were not fulfilling this time allotment. The manpower required for the implementation of the literacy campaign was recruited from among students, schoolteachers and other literate members of the country. However, the qualification of the mustered manpower was later found to be lower than desired. The participation of women was minimal in the administration of the campaign at all levels; however, women composed over 50 per cent of the literacy participants.

Each urban dweller and peasant organization had at least one major literacy centre. In fact, some of the larger organizations had one or more sub-centres due to the large number of enrollees. Right from the beginning, it was recognized that the resources required, especially for classroom facilities, would be in short supply. Thus, the National Literacy Campaign Co-ordinating Committee (NLCCC) issued a guideline saying that literacy would be conducted everywhere, even under the shade of a tree if necessary. The types of facilities in which the literacy classes were conducted varied according to what was available. In some cases, new structures were built for the literacy centre, while in others, meeting halls, formal schools (when they were not being used for formal educational purposes) and other suitable buildings and shelters were utilized. While more than half of the centres had to rely on formal school facilities, none of the established centres was left without a building facility at its disposal.

The major sources of finance for the National Literacy Campaign came from the communities, the government, non-government organizations, and also from bilateral and international donor agencies. Additionally, there was extensive support from the community in the building of literacy centres and in the provision of some of the learning materials. However, the supply of educational materials was still inadequate in many areas.

The instruction was conducted largely with traditional methods such as drilling and group recital, and often lacked the motivational aspect so vital for maintaining participation. The attendance was usually around 50 per cent. While Amharic is recognized as the national language, it was not the only language used in conducting the literacy campaign. In the country as a whole, nearly ninety different languages are spoken, but for matters of practicality only fifteen languages were used in the rural areas. In the urban areas, where the population is quite heterogeneous, only Amharic was used.

6.2 Organization and structure of the evaluation activity

In 1983, it was decided to conduct an evaluation of a summative nature in order to appraise the achievements of the literacy campaign. This Ethiopian Literacy Campaign Evaluation (ELCE) was to be implemented in three phases. The first phase was to assess the campaign's implementation and impact in urban areas. The second phase was to pursue the same objectives, only at a later time and for the rural, rather than the urban, areas. The third and last phase would deal with post-literacy activities in the country. The project was originally designed for a period of thirty months with ten months allotted for each phase. For now, we will concern ourselves with only the first two phases of the ELCE project which have been completed.

In addition to these immediate evaluative interests, the ELCE project reflected a wider interest of the Ministry of Education in the upgrading and strengthening of the national and local research and information-gathering capacity in the field of non-formal education and its relations with the formal system. The ELCE project was funded by the International Development Research Centre (IDRC), a Canadian research organization, to assist the Ethiopian Ministry of Education in organizing and implementing the evaluation of its literacy campaign.

According to the major targets of the NLCCC and the National Literacy Campaign, illiteracy should have been eradicated in the urban areas by 1981, and in the rural areas by 1987. Thus, it was only logical that the first phase of the ELCE project was begun in the urban areas. The first phase of the evaluation should have been completed by June 1983, but due to organizational and research personnel problems, this phase of the project was extended to June 1984. The original time schedule was then adjusted for the remaining two phases of the ELCE project.

The second phase of the project was directed towards an evaluation of the conditions of rural literacy in different environmental and cultural settings. The third and last phase of the project focused on the post-literacy question. It was expected that the experience accrued in the evaluation of the first phase would serve to improve the quality of evaluation of the remaining phases.

Generally, the evaluation project set out to:

> (a) explore ways to improve the data-base required at the district level, to assess the outcomes of the literacy project, verify the validity of data previously collected, and review the possibility of extending the range of those now collected and analyzed; (b) analyze the process and impact of the existing campaign, including how long it takes people to become literate, how functionally literate people are at the end of the campaign, what kinds of mechanisms and skills in training and teaching are being developed in the campaign, and what is being done to retain literacy after formal certification is achieved; and (c) assess what further educational activities should follow the campaign, including how to integrate it with the formal school system and how to build on people's literacy in other programmes and services. (IDRC, 3-P-82-0010, para. 12:5, as cited in Chinapah, 1984:2.)

As is usually the case in many developing countries, Ethiopia was confronted with a number of problems in building its own educational research competence. Among others, there was a great shortage of qualified local educational research personnel and the possibilities for training and upgrading local educational researchers within and outside the country were limited. The country suffered from a poor climate in the planning and execution of educational research projects, as the barriers within and between institutions and departments restricted the type of co-operation and research exchange necessary for the successful implementation of any individual research project. Further, there was a great deal of wastage of the scarce available resources (human, material and financial) due to the stiff competition, the lack of communication and the duplication efforts and work any single research project had to live with.

Thus, the overriding objective of the ELCE project, as indicated in the IDRC document, was to develop the necessary local research competence for the evaluation of the National Literacy Campaign and to provide a conducive climate for further research.

> The funding of this project, therefore should lead both to increased research and management skills in particular regions of Ethiopia and in particular segments of the education system (the literacy campaign), and to a greater understanding of the need for--and possible strategies for achieving--the enhancement of more general capacity in educational research. (IDRC, 3-P-82-0010, para. 12:5, as cited in Chinapah, 1984:2.)

This meant, therefore, that one of the intentions of the ELCE project was to create a better climate for educational research in Ethiopia. Within a broader framework of building educational research competence in the country, this project would contribute to: (a) an increase in trained personnel for future educational research; (b) a demonstration of the application of research findings to policy- and decision-making; (c) the upgrading of equipment and other research facilities; (d) a general awareness of the significance of research, and the methodologies and resources required for its implementation; and (e) the dissemination of information to other countries and organizations engaged in similar operations.

More specifically, the objectives of the ELCE Project were:
A. *Analyse the process, i.e. all activities involved in the implementation of the literacy campaign:*
1. Examine the situation regarding educational materials and physical facilities.
2. Study the contribution of the community.
3. Examine the learning-teaching situation.
4. Estimate how long it takes an adult to become literate.
5. Study the efficiency of the administrative body.

B. *Analyse the impact of the literacy campaign:*
1. Examine how functionally literate people are when they become literate.
2. Estimate the dropout rate and find the reasons for dropping out.
3. Discover whether there is a problem of relapse after certification.
4. Study the benefits acquired through literacy.

C. *Analyse literacy data collected:*
1. Verify the validity of data previously collected.
2. Review the possibility of extending the range of data now collected and analysed.
3. Explore ways to improve the data base required at the district level.

Overall, it was possible to transform the set objectives into operational targets; however, two objectives were not satisfactorily covered by the evaluation (Makonnen, 1987). These concerned: (a) the estimation and analysis of the dropout rate; and (b) the examination of how functionally literate people are when they become literate. The reasons for these shortcomings were, in part, due to missing data and the project design.

Within the general context of the National Literacy Campaign, the ELCE project shed light on the achievements, data-collection system and flow of information from the completed rounds of the campaign, and made use of the results for improving the ongoing literacy campaign and post-literacy programmes. In other words, this project served in the development of an efficient and consistent data-collection framework for the future progress of the literacy campaign, and from the information collected it assisted policy-makers and programme developers in taking the necessary measures for improvements in the remaining rounds of the campaign and in the post-literacy programmes.

The Adult Education Department and the Planning Services of the Ministry of Education were the main co-ordinating bodies in the planning and organization of the project. The involvement of the other institutions such as the Curriculum Department of the Ministry of Education, the Institute of Development Research and the Faculty of Education from Addis Ababa University was marginal. Besides institutional and departmental barriers, the support expected for the ELCE project from local professional and educational research staff was limited. Most of the qualified research personnel were engaged in a nationwide research project commissioned by the state.

A project co-ordinating committee was formed to facilitate the implementation of the ELCE project. It was chaired by the head of the Adult Education Department and included the head of the Planning and External Relations Services and members of the research team. One advantage of the composition of this co-ordinating committee was that it helped to bring together the two mentioned departments, as they collaborated in the provision of manpower and transport for the field-work. The qualification of the manpower generally was good but nobody was highly trained in research methodology. However, the IDRC provided highly qualified consultants from time to time to assist and advise. The executive committee under the co-ordinating committee contained the research unit of the Planning and External Relations Services. It had three subcommittees each with its own responsibilities (Figure 6).

Although the structure of the project was clearly spelled out, the subcommittees were not fully functional due to the limited manpower available. From the description of the duties and responsibilities for each committee and group, a great deal of overlapping could be observed. In such a situation, there is always a danger of a number of duties and responsibilities being duplicated, while the actual tasks are performed by a few interested and motivated members. In the case of the ELCE project, it was observed that these tasks were more or less performed by members of the research team.

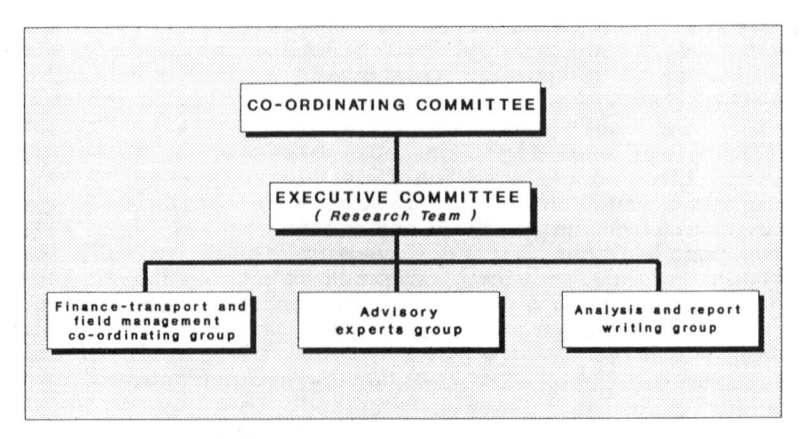

```
                    ┌──────────────────────────┐
                    │  CO-ORDINATING COMMITTEE │
                    └────────────┬─────────────┘
                                 │
                    ┌────────────┴─────────────┐
                    │    EXECUTIVE COMMITTEE   │
                    │      ( Research Team )   │
                    └────────────┬─────────────┘
          ┌──────────────────────┼──────────────────────┐
┌─────────┴─────────┐  ┌─────────┴────────┐  ┌──────────┴─────────┐
│ Finance-transport │  │     Advisory     │  │ Analysis and report│
│    and field      │  │  experts group   │  │   writing group    │
│    management     │  │                  │  │                    │
│ co-ordinating grp │  │                  │  │                    │
└───────────────────┘  └──────────────────┘  └────────────────────┘
```

Fig. 6. The organization of the ELCE project.   After Makonnen (1987:6).

6.3 Evaluation design and coverage

Considering the available resources, the coverage for the ELCE project was perhaps too broad and ambitious right from the start. The research team, which consisted of six members, was actively involved in planning and organization, instrument construction, sampling, field-work and data collection of the first phase of the project. However, due to the wide coverage of the first phase of the project (47 urban literacy centres from 23 districts of the 7 zones) the research team was divided into three groups to carry out the field work and data collection. This division of the team into three groups caused some serious problems for project. A *"laissez-faire* approach" was espoused and as a result the selection of key informants, the data-collection techniques and the key information gathered varied from group to group.

According to the *Research Work Manual* (as cited in Chinapah, 1984:7), within the general framework of this project, the evaluation would focus on the achievements, data-collection system and flow of information in the ongoing literacy campaign and post-literacy programme. The evaluation would consist of both descriptive and analytical designs. A quantitative evaluation research design had been adopted in this project with regard to sampling, instrument construction, selection of key informants and data-collection techniques. This design seemed to have strongly affected the use of the (time, personnel and financial) earmarked for the first phase of the project. For instance, there was not enough time for the analysis of the results from the pilot study due to the wide coverage planned for the field survey.

On the question of sampling of urban literacy centres in Phase I, the design was based on a greater number of centres rather than on their representativeness within the given strata. The questionnaires consisted of a number of open-ended questions, yet such questions could have been dealt with through interviews and observation schedules.

6.4 Evaluation instruments

Several sets of instruments (questionnaires, interviews, observation schedules, documentary studies and cognitive tests) were designed for the ELCE project. Building on experience, they varied slightly in content from Phase I to Phase II. The instruments were addressed to different categories of informants and covered a very wide range of issues. They could be grouped into the following problem areas of the National Literacy Campaign: (a) mass participation and types of mobilization in the campaign; (b) supporting services and infrastructure (the availability of buildings, educational materials and assistance from mass organizations) for the campaign; (c) quality of the teaching-learning environments and processes; (d) provision and use of teaching-learning materials; (e) curriculum and syllabus; (f) didactics, course management and supervision; (g) content, types and methods of data and information system; (h) basic data on reasons for dropout, on measures against relapsing into illiteracy and on benefits accrued from literacy; (i) ability and cognitive skills acquired by adult literates; and (j) linkage of the campaign to the formal school system.

In all, eleven instruments were designed for the collection of the necessary data. Makonnen (1987:11) lists them as follows: (a) three questionnaires (one more for the adult education officer in Phase I); (b) three interview schedules (one group interview schedule was added in Phase II, while the interview schedule on dropouts was abandoned); (c) three observation schedules; (d) one cognitive test; and (e) one document sheet (Phase II only).

The development and construction of these instruments were based on an intensive literature review. In the design of these instruments, the research project team consulted some members of the different committees and teams. For example, the cognitive instruments were developed in close collaboration with experts from the Curriculum Department. For further guidance in the design of the instruments, a big table was utilized that listed the objectives, the hypotheses, the type of item that would be needed to prove or disprove each particular hypothesis, the source of the information and the way it could be obtained. This organizational method was useful as it brought together the various elements mentioned above, and helped to clarify all the aspects of the phenomena under study.

Among the several sets of instruments, the questionnaires were designed to serve as the principal source of information. They were addressed to the chairmen of the local associations, the centre representatives, the adult education officer (Phase I only) and the literacy teachers.

In all three sets of questionnaires, some common items were included in order to map the progress and the problematic of the literacy campaign from rather different perspectives. However, the questionnaires for the local chairmen and the centre representatives contained the bulk of the information. These two sets of questionnaires were somewhat lengthy. They were respectively thirteen and seventeen pages in their English version. The questionnaire for the chairmen focused on issues about the National Literacy Campaign in general, while the questionnaire for the centre representatives dealt much more with the campaign at the literacy centre. The set of questionnaires addressed to the adult education officers at the district level covered management and supervision, training and recruitment of literacy teachers, teaching methods and the availability and use of teaching aids.

Interviews were conducted with adult literacy participants and literacy teachers. In the first phase, there were two categories of adult literacy participants. The first category consisted of beginners from the 10th round who dropped out in the 9th round of the campaign. A short interview was designed for them and focused on the major causes of why they had dropped out from the 9th round. The second category consisted of adult literates who had participated in the 2nd, 5th and 8th rounds of the campaign. The interview included some selected background characteristics on the informants and the possibilities provided for them for continuing education, such as reading rooms and reading materials. In the literacy centre, literacy teachers were selected according to their subject area for interviews concerning information on the teaching aids and the teaching-learning interactions with adult literacy participants.

The interview schedules varied slightly for the second phase. In the second phase, interviews were held with the adult participants, both individually and in groups, both for those who had completed the cognitive test and for those who where still participating in the literacy classes. A semi-structured open interview schedule was also used in this phase in order to obtain qualitative information regarding individual and societal benefits, as well as future needs. The first interview schedule was used to gather views from the newly literate adults on the impact of literacy. The second was directed to adults presently attending literacy in the beginners' or remedial programmes, with the purpose of acquiring information on the learning-teaching situation, on reasons for absenteeism and tardiness and on adults' motivation to participate in the literacy campaign. The third interview schedule was used to collect background information from adults who took the cognitive test. The purpose was to find out how they applied the skills they acquired up to the time they took the cognitive test.

The cognitive test was used to measure the literate adults' present skill in three areas: (a) reading comprehension; (b) ability to express their ideas in writing (this often involved simple letter-writing); and (c) arithmetic, which usually involved simple calculations. The test was designed to find out whether the adults were qualified in accordance with Unesco's definition of a literate person, which is essentially the ability to read and write with understanding, and the ability to understand and use the four computations of arithmetic.

The two remaining types of instrument, the observation schedule and the documentary study, were designed for cross-checking purposes. They were structured in such a way as to account for the actual progress and problematics of the campaign at the literacy centre. Among others, the conditions at the centre, the availability and use of teaching and learning materials, the preparation of a timetable, the records for attendance, the type of data and information system, and the extension services for post-literacy programmes were recorded. The three observation schedules covered the learning-teaching atmosphere in the classroom, the system used in the collection of data and its quality at the centre and district levels. The document sheet was used to collect data on class attendance for six different months in two rounds, the purpose being mainly to estimate average attendance and examine it for different seasons.

The instruments were tested in a pilot study which was conducted in three towns prior to the start of the first phase. These towns were selected according to their degree of urbanization. As there was no written documentation on the pilot study, the information was provided through discussions with the research project team. Unfortunately, due to time constraints, the outcomes from the pilot study were not studied in detail and no in-depth analysis of the instruments (formats, phrasing, clarity, etc.) was made. This exercise would have reduced, for example, the numerous open-ended questions in the different sets of questionnaires. Many difficult and unreliable questions would have been discarded. In other words, the quality and reliability of the instruments could have been greatly improved.

Thus, for the first phase, the sets of instruments were too bulky and contained few qualitative types of data. Much more emphasis should have been given to the preparation of the instruments (improvement in their formats and phrasing). The results from the pilot study should have been properly studied in order to serve such purposes. These instruments were improved and modified for the second phase. The questions were designed to be more direct and succinct, and were directed to more appropriate informants. Also more effective changes were made in the cognitive test for Phase II.

6.5 Target population and sampling procedures

For the first phase, a multi-stage sampling design was used. The first sampling stage consisted of a selection of towns. The towns were grouped into three strata according to the size of their population. They were: (a) small towns with a population between 2,000 and 10,000; (b) medium towns with a population between 10,001 and 25,000; and (c) large towns with a population greater than 25,000. In each zone, 4 towns were selected (2 small, 1 medium and 1 large). In the second sampling stage, urban literacy centres were randomly selected. The number of centres selected from each stratum was as follows: 1 centre in small towns; 2 centres in medium towns; and 3 centres in large towns. There were altogether 26 towns (11 small, 8 medium and 7 large) in the sample. Data were available from 47 of the 52 designated urban literacy centres, of which 10 were from small towns, 16 from medium towns and 21 from large towns.

The reasons advocated for a judgmental sampling of towns in the first phase were that it would be more costly and time-consuming if these towns were randomly selected. However, it is not certain that these reasons are valid as random sampling fulfills the same purpose. The decision to include most of the big towns in the sampling caused additional problems when generalizing the results to the target population. A further improvement of the sampling design could have been made if the information about the number of urban literacy centres in each stratum was used.

Once the urban literacy centres were sampled, some further sampling was required for the informants. However, while the literacy teachers from each centre were selected by subject areas, the adult literacy participants were randomly selected. As mentioned earlier, there were two groups of adult literacy participants: (a) those who were beginners in the 10th round but dropouts of the 9th round; and (b) those who were adult literates from the 2nd, 5th and 8th rounds. In the first group, 10 informants were randomly selected from each centre while in the second group, 10 informants from each of the three rounds were randomly selected. In the sampling of these two categories of informants, sex and age characteristics were not considered, this type of personal data being collected later.

The sample coverage could have been significantly reduced without any damage to the scope and objectives of the field survey. The selection of fewer towns and urban literacy centres through an appropriate sampling design would have provided more qualitative results from the field survey within the same amount of resources earmarked. For instance, more time could have been spent on the analysis of the results from the pilot study, the improvement of instruments and data-collection techniques (including a wider range of qualitative data) and in-depth discussion with members assigned to each group of the field survey.

Phase II sampling was different, however. The sampling procedure was determined by taking into consideration the maximum time allowed for the field-work and the travel costs involved. The sampling design was to produce the best possible sample of adults for a cognitive test. Care was taken that the number of peasant associations represented would not be less than 20. With respect to the limitations, cluster sampling was decided upon. The sampling procedure was in three stages: (a) the selection of districts; (b) the selection of a peasant association from each district; and (c) the selection of individuals.

Stratification was also carried out as all districts of the included regions were divided into strata, using nationality language in the district, crop type and primary school distribution as stratification factors. These factors were chosen for sampling on the assumption that they affected the implementation of the literacy programme in rural areas in different ways. Further, the individuals were stratified according to the round in which they received their certificate. Half of the participants sampled were from the early rounds and half from the later rounds.

The sample was designed to contain 24 peasant associations from different districts, and from each association, 10 adults for the cognitive test. The actual sample was then drawn with the use of proportionate sampling, with the probability of a district being represented in the sample proportionate to its total number of peasant association members out of the whole stratum. When the sample was drawn, one district had to be replaced by another similar district from the same stratum in order to reduce the costs for the field-work. For each sample district, a reserve was chosen. The stratified cluster sampling had worked fairly well; however, the distribution of primary schools served no purpose, probably because the definition used did not consider distance between schools and peasant associations.

6.6 Data collection

For the first phase, the field-work and data-collection activities were carried out by three groups. The groups consisted of members of the research team. The first group covered the north, north-west and western zones; the second group covered the central, eastern and southern zones; and the third group covered Addis Ababa. During the five days allocated for field-work and data collection in each town, the questionnaires were filled in and returned, while the interviews, tests, observation schedules and documentary studies were carried out.

Although the urban literacy centres were informed in advance about the field survey, the time-schedule was kept secret in order to avoid extra preparation and to map the actual state of affairs at the centre. The selection and sampling of adult literacy participants were made on the spot. The selected adult literacy participants were then told to be present on the third day for an interview. Tests in reading comprehension, letter-writing and simple calculation were administered in each centre for the sampled adult literates from the 2nd, 5th and 8th rounds. During the first and the last day of the field survey, meetings were organized with members of the urban dweller association literacy campaign committee at each centre.

As has been mentioned, a *laissez-faire* approach was adopted by the three groups of the research team during the field-work and data-collection activities. There were many implications in the use of such an approach, not least, the processing and analysis of the data collected. Three fundamental problems were identified. First, observation schedules were carried out differently. In some centres, the entire group made one observation schedule while in other centres each member of the group made his own observation schedule. Second, the interview with literacy teachers was conducted in different ways. One group of the research team had chosen for their interview one literacy teacher to represent the centre instead of applying the design which called for interviews at the centre with literacy teachers by subject areas. This implies that some centres had more data from literacy teachers than others. Third, socio-economic data were collected by only one of the three groups on the sample of adults who had dropped out in the 9th round of the campaign. As the data from the field survey had to be analysed for the entire sample, this *laissez-faire* approach had to be taken into consideration during the interpretation of results.

The application of different data-collection techniques was tested during the pilot study. It was observed that it was not possible to have direct interviews with adult literacy participants on issues related to the organizational structure, nature and content, and problems concerning the National Literacy Campaign. The first obstacle was the actual presence of the research project team. The informants found it difficult to communicate with the investigators in the presence of their colleagues. They were quiet in most cases. Second, the questions asked were too sensitive. There was a tendency among the active informants to present their own personal and socio-economic problems instead of responding to questions about the literacy campaign. Third, the research project team had not tried any alternative methods of tackling the problems encountered (conducting individual interviews instead of group interviews, acting as observers on interviews carried out through the literacy teachers, and so on).

There was a combination of too many data-collection techniques in the field survey, serving sometimes similar purposes, e.g. questionnaires and interviews. More qualitative types of data could have been collected through interviews and observation schedules. The documentary studies could have focused on basic data about the National Literacy Campaign and similar data at the literacy centre level. This strategy would have compensated for the amount of missing information on questionnaires from the association chairmen and the centre representatives, and would have allowed a better use of the time for the collection of qualitative types of data through interviews and observation schedules.

The above-mentioned problems were considered in Phase II and the decision was made to use only the literacy teachers as informants on the teaching-learning interactions. Some alternative methods could have been tried first before the exclusion of adult literacy participants on general matters concerning the literacy campaign and on the teaching-learning processes. In short, the lack of relevant information from the actual beneficiaries of the literacy campaign destroyed the quality of the first phase of this evaluation project.

For the second phase, five groups were involved in the data collection. There were some inconsistencies in the way in which the instruments were administered among the teams, but overall, the quality of the data collected was good. These inconsistencies resulted, in part, because of the large number of teams used and the differences in research ability among them. These groups had asked that the educational offices involved collect the necessary information prior to the field-work; however, this was completed to varying extents, and in some places not at all.

Data were collected with varying collection forms prepared at differing levels, and this resulted in missing and inconsistent data. Sometimes data were not collected, or were lost at the centre level, and often the data collected did not include demographic information which was necessary to assist in future planning activities.

Makonnen (1987:13) lists a few other problems encountered in the data collection: (a) the non-existence of systematically recorded data in some literacy centres; (b) the non-comparability of data kept at the centre and other levels; (c) the difficulty of finding literacy centres that met the sample criteria; and (d) the adults' reluctance to give information that they considered would incriminate others.

In both phases, prior to the field-work, workshops were conducted on the administering of the instruments. The workshops covered the work programme and the techniques of administering different kinds of instruments, with an emphasis on the method of interviewing and the presentation of the cognitive test. The intention of the workshops was to acquaint the new field-workers with the aims of the study and to make sure that the different groups administered all instruments in a similar manner, thus reducing the possibility of "interviewer errors" as much as possible. The workshops were accompanied by field manuals which specified in detail the activities and the procedure of work to be followed in the field.

6.7 Analytical strategy

The analysis in the ELCE project was mostly descriptive. What was attempted was to assess the educational input, the process, and finally the output, in both quantitative and qualitative dimensions. The analytical part of the study resulted from the cognitive test given to adult participants for the purpose of examining how far they were able to retain the skills they acquired. The approach of analysis was similar in the first two phases.

In Ethiopia, as in many developing countries today, the competence and skills required for the processing and analysis of the massive amount of existing data are very limited. One fundamental problem has been the distance created between two tight stages of an educational evaluation project, namely the data-collection stage and the data-processing and -analysis stage. The first phase of the ELCE project was confronted with a similar problem right from the beginning.

During the processing and analysis of the data, the following activities were carried out: (a) design of a conceptual model for the analysis of the data collected; (b) sorting and screening of the reliable and valid data; (c) development of code-books and the creation of separate files for each category of informant; (d) preparation of the format for, and the planning of, different types of analysis; (e) detailed examination of the types of results from the analysis and their interpretation; and (f) elaboration of the report.

The conceptual model. It was understood that an intensive literature review was to be made during the design of this evaluation research project. Such a review should have, among other things, contributed to the development of a conceptual model guiding all stages of the evaluation. The major purpose of a conceptual model is to help in: (a) the formulation of hypotheses; (b) the development and construction of relevant instruments; (c) the selection of key concepts and variables; and (d) the planning of relevant types of analysis.

At its outset, the ELCE project was not guided by any conceptual model. As a result, severe difficulties were encountered during the planning of the data-processing and data-analysis stages of the evaluation. Formidable questions arose that could not easily be resolved, such as: How to treat the massive amount of data collected? Do all these data necessarily address the objectives set up in this evaluation? Can these concepts be empirically examined from the information collected? If so, what kinds of analysis are appropriate? In brief, one can see how imperative it was to link the various stages of the evaluation project, i.e. from project objectives and instrument construction, to data processing and data analysis.

Later, a conceptual model was tentatively adopted which focused principally on the relation between the data that had already been collected and the objectives set up in the evaluation (Figure 7). The model was then used for the identification of key concepts and variables from the different sets of instruments. It was also used later in the design of the various types of analysis.

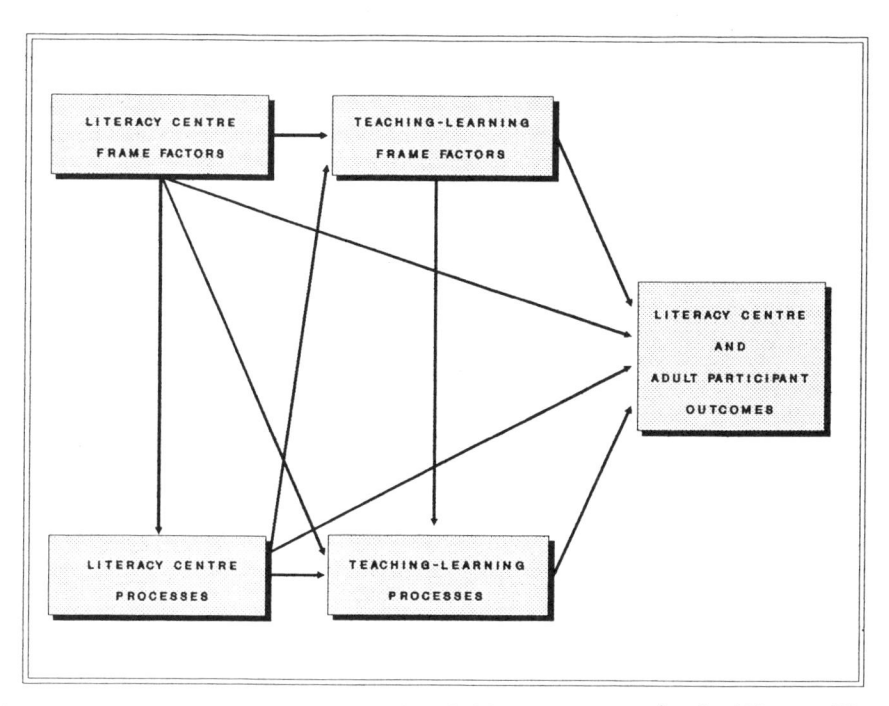

Fig. 7. The conceptual model of the ELCE project (Phase I). After Chinapah (1984:17).

In this conceptual model, three categories of data were selected: (a) those related to the frame factors; (b) those related to processes; and (c) those related to outcomes. The frame factors consisted of basic and crude indicators describing the environmental setting of the urban literacy centres and the teaching-learning conditions. Processes focused on what actually took place at the centre and in the respective classes. Lastly, outcomes were measured from both the literacy centre perspective and the individual adult literacy participant perspective. They included crude outcomes of the campaign at the level of the literacy centre (passes, failures, dropouts, repeaters and community development) and individual outcomes at the level of the adult literacy participant (performance on cognitive tests for those in the 2nd, 5th and 8th rounds and participation in post-literacy programmes and in mass organizations).

The model of analysis, developed more specifically for Phase II of the evaluation, varied slightly from the conceptual model adopted for Phase I. Figure 8 outlines this model more clearly.

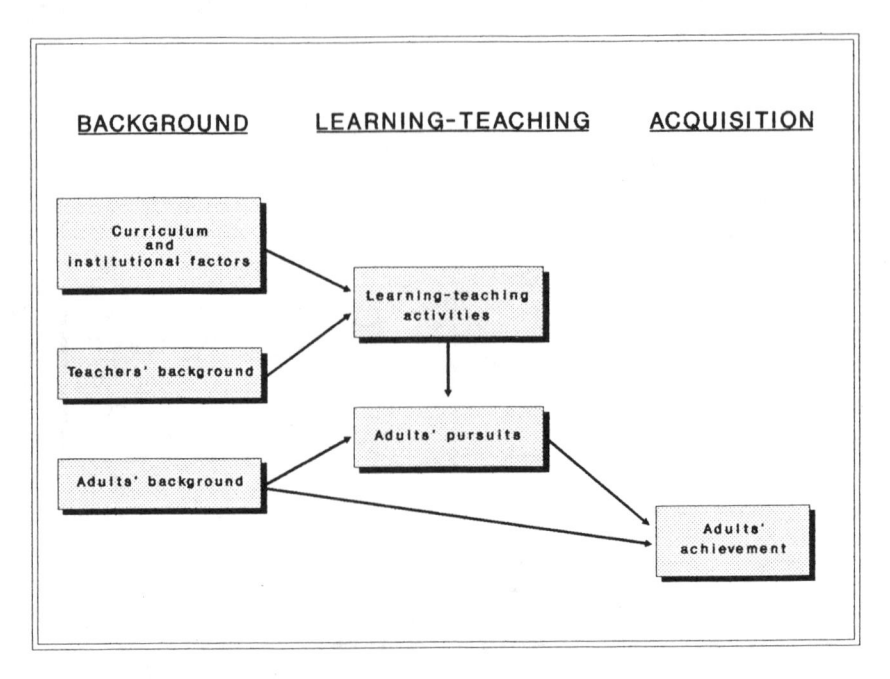

Fig. 8. Analytical model of the ELCE project (Phase II). After Makonnen (1987:10).

From this analytical model, five blocks of different variables were constructed: (a) adults' background; (b) adults' pursuits; (c) centre characteristics (curriculum, institutional factors and teachers' background); (d) learning-teaching activities; and (e) adults' achievement. The design of the analysis was intended to be based on this model; however, the study had not been an experimental one where the adults were followed throughout their literacy training, thus it was not possible to apply the model fully. Relating the learning-teaching situation to the adults' achievements was nearly impossible as the adults had finished their course and acquired the skills in earlier rounds while the learning-teaching process was studied in a later round.

The third Block (c), the centre characteristics, could not be considered either due to a lack of proper documentation. The attempt here was therefore limited to analysing the effect of time on the adults' acquired skills and the factors contributing to the effect. This was analysed by comparing adults who obtained their literacy certificate in two different periods. In effect, it meant concentrating the analysis on blocks (a), (b) and (e).

Sorting and screening procedure. The data from the different sets of instruments were studied item-wise. In order to facilitate the item analysis, the data was recorded on tally sheets for each individual set of instruments. The sorting and screening procedure focused then on: (a) the relevance of the data; (b) the quality of the responses; and (c) the amount of missing data for each item. In all three cases, the basic problem was actually the nature and quality of the instruments used in the field survey (see Chinapah, 1984). Although the objectives set for this evaluation were very ambitious, a significant amount of data collection was serving unspecified purposes. After the cross-examination of the battery of instruments, the irrelevant items were discarded, in some cases because they were redundant.

The format and phrasing of many questions were unclear. In the absence of instructions, the informants had great difficulty in responding to the questions asked; thus there was a great deal of inconsistency in the responses given. In such a situation, only valid data were tallied. A greater problem was found from the responses given to open-ended questions. For instance, it was observed from the frequency table that out of 47 respondents, some 15 to 20 alternative responses were given to a single item on the questionnaire. These responses had to be sorted out and structured into a few interrelated variables.

It was quite obvious from the instruments that much of the information expected from the informants would be missing. In this context, these instruments could have been revised after the pilot study. However, such an exercise was not performed and the end result was a severe shortage of expected data from the instruments used in the field survey. Items with more than 70 per cent non-response were discarded from further analysis. The frequency distribution of the selected items was studied and the responses were reorganized in a limited number of categories. Every single item from the sets of instruments was studied in light of the project objectives. The items were then organized into relevant concepts for analysis.

The sorting and screening procedure had significantly reduced the amount of data available for further analysis. In a similar vein, it had shed light on various aspects of the survey, including the types and quality of information available on the National Literacy Campaign in the urban areas. Such an exercise was extremely useful for the remaining phases of the ELCE project, namely for the improvement in the design of the instruments (format and phrasing), and for the possible better use of a combination of different data-collection techniques.

In both phases, all the completed instruments were carefully reviewed (once together with the respective group) in order to check data for consistency. In the first phase, the major part of the data processing was done manually, while in the second phase, all the data were entered into a computer and double-checked, once through checking against the instruments and another time after frequency tabulation, when some inconsistencies in the original data were found. The open-ended questions had been compiled manually. The computer was then used for all the tabulation and analysis work as well as for the production of some graphics. For the statistical work, the software Systat was used.

Code-books and file building. Code-books were prepared for each individual set of instruments. They consisted of the basic information required for any type of data analysis. These code-books can serve analysis based on either simple calculators or statistical packages for computer use (e.g. SPSS or SAS). In the sets of code-books used, information was provided on: (a) the question number in the instruments; (b) the variable name; (c) the range for each variable minimum and maximum; (d) the missing value code; and (e) the value label, i.e. the description of the value attached to each variable. It should be noted that these code-books had been developed after the item analysis in the first phase. This implied that some items, including particular types of response, were excluded before the development of these code-books.

The file-building exercise was adjusted to the SPSS computer programme that was available at the Central Statistics Office (CSO), whose computer facilities were utilized. The files included the basic information for the use of this programme. Separate files were built for each set of instruments. It was agreed that these would be merged into one single file only when the analysis was performed across different data sets.

The Strategy of Analysis. For the first phase, the strategy of analysis was oriented towards the conceptual model adopted. It is important to note that at this stage the data from the tally sheets could have been further analysed by simple calculators (frequencies, means, cross-tabulations and so on). However, the task would have been an enormous one. In the end, a strategy for the analysis using the SPSS programme was worked out. All the data were transferred on to coding sheets, and these coding sheets - together with code-books and samples of files - were submitted to the computer division at the CSO where they were studied in depth.

The SPSS manual was used in the training/upgrading sessions with the evaluation project team and was later used as a reference for the continuation of the analytical work. The training/upgrading sessions were oriented towards the following statistical programmes: (a) condescriptive; (b) cross-tabulation and breakdown; (c) simple regression analysis; (d) analysis of variance; and (e) multiple regression analysis. The inputs for, and the outputs from, these programmes were studied in detail.

The experience from the training/upgrading sessions was then put into practice. The evaluation project team was assigned to select some key variables from the first phase of the ELCE project and to plan for their appropriate types of analysis. The results were then sent to the computer division of the CSO for actual data-processed analysis. For immediate purposes, only condescriptive, cross-tabulation, breakdown and simple regression (Pearson Corr) programmes were used. The remaining types of analysis, which deserve more in-depth preparation and which require an improved competence in instrument construction and evaluation design, had to wait till the later phases of the ELCE project.

For the second phase, the analysis work started with the designing of a table in which all the hypotheses were written one by one horizontally while all information collected from the different instruments was listed vertically. In the cells of the table, the hypotheses were linked with the relevant data for testing. The analytical work itself was performed in a traditional manner starting with frequency tabulation of all the variables. This was done before the outline for the report was drafted in order to have a basic knowledge of the material first. Then, tables, cross-tables, means and standard deviations were produced stepwise and the significance test performed (for the section concerned with the effects of the literacy campaign, this was followed by studies of covariation and correlation and finally a multiple regression approach).

The structure of the report. One of the major aims of the report from Phase I was to highlight the evaluation experiences from the first phase and the improvements required for the planning, design and implementation of the remaining phases of the ELCE project. The report provided a backdrop to the project as well as a detailed account of the various evaluation activities performed. It highlighted the extent to which the objectives had been reached, and emphasized the strengths and weaknesses perceived during the planning and implementation. The report also contained the major results from the urban literacy campaign and their interpretations, as well as provided recommendations that served as a guideline for the remaining phases of the ELCE project. On the basis of previous experience, it emphasized the need to delimit the sample coverage and to improve the quality of the instruments and the data-collection techniques. It also touched upon the additional assistance required for the remaining phases in: (a) the design of the new instruments; (b) the sampling of the centres and key informants; (c) the choice of appropriate data techniques; and (d) the processing and analysis of the data to be collected (Chinapah, 1984).

For the report from Phase II, an outline was first elaborated which comprised a short description of the content and a detailed reference to the different sources of information for each chapter and section. The outline served as an integrator for the report which was produced with computer support. The method used had been to analyse data in the statistical programme, read-in selected results into the integrator framework and complete it with interpretive text. Step by step then, the integrator was built out to the complete report. This method of report writing had many advantages as it saved time and reduced the sources of error.

Despite the difficult conditions under which the ELCE project had to operate, the evaluation team had generally succeeded in this challenging and innovative evaluation endeavour. The collaborative work had enabled a proper diagnosis of major problems concerning the research activities performed, and provided the skills and experience required for the development and improvement of the evaluation competence in Ethiopia. Most important to the literacy campaign, however, was the knowledge and feedback gained which helped to improve the ongoing literacy efforts. This information and experience will be of great use in future literacy and educational planning.

In the coming chapter, we shall discuss the experience from the evaluation of industrial education in academic secondary schools in Kenya. This evaluation incorporates a series of studies using both cross-sectional and longitudinal designs. Much of the discussion in this chapter will focus on the application of the different principles and practices in evaluating programmes and projects in the area of technical/vocational education presented in Chapter 4. We believe that the experience from the evaluation of industrial education in academic secondary schools in Kenya will complement the two other evaluation experiences. Together, these three evaluation experiences serve as relevant inputs for the understanding and interpretation of the pragmatic domain in our holistic approach to educational evaluation.

7. The Evaluation Study of Industrial Education in Academic Secondary Schools in Kenya

7.1 The Industrial Education project in Kenya

Technical/vocational education in Kenyan schools can trace its roots back to its colonial past when handicrafts was a subject offered in many secondary schools. After independence in 1963, some schools continued to offer courses in woodwork, metalwork and geometrical and mechanical drawing, but as was common in many developing countries, vocational education was largely perceived as an inferior type of education.

The need for manpower during this early period was satisfied through general secondary education and other types of education. However, with the rapid economic growth in the late 1960s and the first half of the 1970s, there was a growing need for more technical and specialized manpower, and it also became more difficult for school-leavers with general a secondary education diploma to find a job. To meet these demands and in order to accommodate the changes taking place, three important steps were taken in 1968 which had a particular influence upon the vocationalization of secondary education in Kenya:
1. The Ministry of Education decided upon a syllabus with the title, "Industrial Arts Interim Scheme for Secondary Schools".
2. The Kenya Science Teacher College (KSTC) was created with the aim of training teachers for technical/vocational subjects at secondary level.
3. The Kenya Institute of Education was established. One of its functions was to edit and test curricula and syllabuses, including those for industrial education.

Shortly after this time, technical/vocational subjects were introduced into general lower and upper secondary education. Industrial Education (IE) became a compulsory subject in Forms I and II of general secondary education and could be chosen freely in Forms III and IV (later it became one of the subjects in the Kenyan Certificate of Education (KCE), the secondary education examination). In relation to the selection to upper secondary and further studies, IE was of the same status as the other subjects.

IE included four branches: wood technology, metal technology, power mechanics technology and electrical technology. Each school was to offer only two of the branches. The recommended time allocation for IE was six periods per week with at least four of these being practical sessions.

The general objectives of IE in Kenya were stated by Lauglo (1985:9) in the following way:
1. To develop in each pupil an insight and an understanding of industry and its place in our society.
2. To discover and develop personal talents in industrial technical fields.
3. To develop problem-solving abilities related to the materials and processes of industry using an applied workshop approach.
4. To develop in each pupil a skill in the safe use and care of tools and machines.
5. To develop in each pupil an awareness of how he, as a consumer, can be efficient in the selection, care and use of industrial products.

A review of the particular IE syllabuses, coursework schedules and examination procedures (which we shall not include in this chapter) reveals that IE was to be pre-vocational and was not primarily intended to lead to an occupation. The main features of the specific objectives and syllabuses for each IE subject have been revised only slightly over the years.

In Kenya, there evolved several variations within the academic curriculum in secondary schools. Some of the academic secondary schools offered options such as agriculture, commerce, home economics or industrial education. Also, in the separate technical secondary schools, both technical and academic subjects were combined, but with more of a vocational rather than a pre-vocational syllabus. In recent years, Kenya has introduced some structural reforms in education; however, the government is still committed to introducing practical subjects on a large scale both in the new eight-year extended primary cycle and in the new four-year secondary cycle.

In this chapter we shall review the evaluation of the Kenya-Sweden Technical and Industrial Education Project (KS), which was conducted in 35 academic secondary schools. This KS project was established in mid-1975 and received Swedish support until 1981. Perhaps it is also important to note that the project only affected 35 out of the more than 800 government-supported schools in Kenya; thus it had a relatively small impact.

The original aims of the KS project were stated by Lauglo (1985:28) as follows:
1. To strengthen Kenyan efforts to introduce a practical element in general academic education.
2. To improve preconditions for teaching IE in twenty-nine secondary schools in accordance with the 1972 syllabuses.
3. To equip these schools adequately so that students were given the opportunity to obtain the required complete experience for the examination in the subject.

4. To achieve, in the short run, a balance between the supply and demand of teachers in IE.

Later the number of schools was extended from 29 to 35. In the Agreement signed in 1974 between Kenya and Sweden, the following components were included:
1. Enlargement and modernization of IE workshops at approximately 30 general secondary schools.
2. Construction of approximately 36 staff houses for IE teachers.
3. Purchase of equipment for the workshops.
4. Strengthening of the capacity of the Ministry of Education.
5. A research programme.

In a broader perspective, Sweden has assisted technical/vocational education in Kenya for nearly twelve years; the KS project is only one part of this long-running co-operation between the two countries in this area. During this twelve-year period, Swedish support has had the following four elements:
1. Teacher education for IE at the Kenya Science Teacher College (KSTC).
2. Swedish volunteer teachers to set up equipment in the workshops and to teach IE courses.
3. Building or renovating and equipping of workshops as well as the construction of some housing for IE teachers.
4. Establishing a maintenance unit that should, *inter alia*, provide support for IE programmes and their workshops.

It is important to draw a distinction between the Technical Secondary Schools (TSS) and the IE project in the academic secondary schools. The KS project dealt with IE, and is largely encompassed in the third element (listed above) of Swedish aid. The TSS also received Swedish support and were evaluated in a similar fashion shortly after the IE evaluation. However, as pointed out above, the evaluation we are concerned with here involves IE in the 35 Swedish-assisted academic secondary schools.

7.2 Background to the evaluation study

The area of vocationalization and curriculum diversification has attracted much international attention in recent years. As pointed out in Chapter 4, the direction of vocational education is widely debated, yet still lacks in-depth evaluations. Thus, one of the aims of this relatively extensive evaluation was its contribution, internationally, to the ongoing question of technical/vocational education in developing countries.

The Swedish International Development Authority (SIDA) engaged the London Institute of Education, University of London, to make an in-depth evaluation of the Swedish-sponsored IE project in Kenya. The evaluation team consisted of seven members with various professional backgrounds; they came from the United Kingdom, Sweden and Kenya.

According to the evaluation project leader, the evaluation was intended for three categories of people: (a) Kenyan politicians and civil servants (at least within the area of education); (b) SIDA officials; and (c) participants in the international debate on the vocationalization of secondary education (Lauglo, 1985). The aims of the evaluation were defined as follows:

1. To identify the aims and objectives of IE in Kenya, to examine these in the Kenyan and international contexts and to trace the main influences on the evolution of aims, objectives and syllabuses.
2. To assess the degree of success of IE both in terms of its official objectives and in terms of the expectations which are held by students, teachers, headmasters, parents and employers. Also, to identify unanticipated outcomes of IE.
3. To identify the conditions which have influenced the degree of success of IE, and to identify the main difficulties or problems pertaining to it, as perceived by those involved in implementing IE or by those directly affected by IE subjects.
4. To examine the cost of IE as compared with other parts of general secondary education and with vocational training.
5. To assess the future role of IE in the schools, within the framework of present educational policy in Kenya.
6. To assess Swedish aid to IE in the light of the general aims for SIDA's work and to suggest guidelines for SIDA with respect to possible future involvement with similar curriculum change in other countries.

Since SIDA was very involved in the IE project and had initiated and financed the evaluation project, and since influence from international agencies should be (and is in the present evaluation) one important factor in an evaluation, the general goals and objectives of the Swedish co-operation with - and aid to - developing countries will be mentioned briefly. Swedish assistance is intended to contribute to the following: (a) economic growth; (b) economic and social equality; (c) political and economic independence; and (d) democratic development.

The evaluation project had a wide scope and domain; its perspective was more holistic than atomistic, more substantive than formalistic and it took overt or latent conflicts and contradictions into consideration. It covered a large domain, although the indicators for some areas are the subjective views and beliefs of those concerned instead of inter-subjective and outside indicators.

In order to clarify various aspects of the evaluation study and to describe it in relation to the schemes or models that were presented in Chapter 4, Table 8 will be used as a point of departure for the presentation of the evaluation study. The evaluation included the following elements or areas:

Table 8. Model for the evaluation study.

1. Localization of the project schools. 2. The IE schools in comparison to other technical/vocational schools. 3. Students and their characteristics and background. 4. Parents' view of IE.
INDUSTRIAL EDUCATION 5. Objectives of the programmes. 6. Teaching staff. 7. Teaching methods. 8. Workshops. 9. Students' attitudes before leaving the school. 10. Costs
PERFORMANCE INDICATORS 11. Students' careers and destinations. 12. Employers' view of IE.

All the points listed in the table were more or less covered in the evaluation. In addition to these points, the international arena, the policies and activities of the concerned agencies and the trends of vocationalization of secondary education were analysed. Further, a brief analysis was drawn up between the relationship of the Kenyan development policy and Kenyan society on the one hand, and the IE project on the other.

In relation to the overview presented in Chapter 4, some aspects or areas are penetrated in depth (the achievement of the students and their examination results, for instance), while other aspects or areas may be said to be missing or under-emphasized. Some of the latter include: (a) the national development objectives and goals and IE in relation to indicators of performance; (b) the recruitment and selection of students with respect to geographical and ethnic background; (c) a direct analysis of the examination system, and thus, of the skills produced in relation to the need for manpower; and (d) the manpower system itself, job opportunities within the relevant sectors and the productivity and competence of the employed ex-students in comparison to those of others (non-IE people) in the same occupations.

7.3 Evaluation design and sampling procedures

The design included tracer studies, surveys (questionnaires to ex-students, headmasters, IE teachers, other teachers, parents, etc.), interviews (with students, ex-students, parents, employers, etc.), participatory observation (in the classes and the workshops), reviews of documents, and so on. The sources came principally from: documents, examination results, information from Kenyan and SIDA officials, students, teachers and headmasters.

The quantitative analysis was based on examination results

in primary and secondary education and answers to the questionnaires. It proceeded from bivariate techniques (cross-tabulations and correlation analysis) to multivariate analysis (regression analysis). The qualitative analysis was based on answers in interviews and observation schemes. The presentation of the qualitative data was mainly combined with that of quantitative data.

A good deal of the data were qualitative in the sense that they were based on attitudes, opinions and beliefs of those concerned (teachers, headmasters, parents, etc.). For example, the skills produced in IE were never measured directly and in relation to manpower needs but were established through indicators of the following type: opinions from the teachers and headmasters, degree of employability and examination results.

The evaluation activities were many, and, as pointed out above, they covered both qualitative and quantitative areas. Below is an approximate chronological ordering of these evaluation activities (Lauglo, 1985:2):

Major Steps in the Evaluation
1. Documentary analysis of IE aims and objectives.
2. Analysis of present educational policy in Kenya - aspects of direct relevance for the IE evaluation project.
3. Review of international literature.
4. Surveys of students: (a) tracing (autumn 1983) those who in earlier years sat for the KCE exam in IE at three different secondary schools; (b) questionnaire survey (autumn 1983) of 1,642 students in 20 schools (15 IE schools), comparing students with varying degree of exposure to IE; (c) a one-year follow-up of students surveyed at the 20 schools; and (d) tracing (summer 1984) students who in 1974 sat for the KCE in IE at one of the involved schools.
5. Tracer survey of Swedish former IE teachers (January-March, 1984).
6. Examination Analysis: (a) comparison of IE schools in terms of results in IE and academic subjects. Comparison of IE schools as a group with other secondary schools, using results in academic subjects up to 1982; and (b) using individual-level data, comparing students taking different IE subjects with students not taking IE at the KCE exam, and with students taking other practical subjects in terms of exam results in English and mathematics.
7. Survey of employers in Nairobi area who were known to have hired former IE students (field-work in August-September 1984).
8. Cost analysis (August 1984).
9. Documentary analysis: the evolution of IE syllabuses, relationship between IE and other post-primary practical or vocational education (Autumn 1984).

Thirty-five secondary schools were involved in the project. The characteristics of the 35 schools were compared with those of other IE schools with respect to: (a) geographical distribution; (b) school status indicated by the primary school examination results and results from the secondary examinations; and (c) school status as indicated by the quality of the buildings and the equipment.

Fifteen of the 35 schools were sampled (more or less a stratified sample). Another 5 schools (outside the project) were selected as "control" schools. All IE students of these schools (in Form IV in 1983) were interviewed before the examination in 1983 and then, one year after the examination, they were asked to fill out a questionnaire.

All sampled students were divided into three categories: (a) those who chose IE voluntarily as a subject in Forms III and IV, and in the final examination; (b) those who had IE in Forms I and II (compulsory) and then chose not to take it in the last two forms; and (c) students from general secondary education.

In all, 1,642 students were interviewed in 1983. One year later (in the follow-up study) 1,080 (70 per cent) of them were traced and answered the questionnaire. Second-hand information (from other students) was gathered on an additional 240 students. In a follow-up in 1986, 314 of the ex-students answered another questionnaire. In the following sections we shall look a little more closely at these activities, especially as they relate to the specific evaluation areas highlighted in each section.

7.4 Evaluation of the project content

It will be recalled that in Chapter 4, we referred to content as an internal aspect of a project or programme, which related to the following: (a) the structure of the system; (b) the curriculum; (c) the teacher quality; (d) the teaching methods and the material framework for teaching/learning; and (e) the examination system.

Besides the obvious questions arising, there were other questions concerning the project content. These included:
1. Is IE perceived more as a pre-vocational subject, preparing students for practical work? Or is it perceived more as a general education subject that is mainly of private use, or useful for subjects regardless of further education or occupational destination?
2. Is IE taught in a highly didactic manner so that students, even in their practical work, are given a series of set tasks that stress precision in execution rather than problem-solving?
3. Do teachers of IE feel constrained by the high specificity of the IE syllabuses? Would they prefer more autonomy in deciding what to teach? Or would they prefer the syllabuses to spell out in even greater detail what should be taught?
4. How satisfied are teachers of IE with the "0 level" examination in IE subjects? Is the balance between theoretical and practical work right? Do they see the exam as a fair one? Do they see it as a straightjacket that prevents them from pursuing the general education aims of IE?

5. Given the official orientation of IE towards "modern industry", with the implications of expensively equipped workshops, do headmasters and IE teachers see a need to simplify the workshop technology in the future development of IE, orienting IE more towards the informal sector of small-scale craft production, if IE were to be expanded to many more schools? Or would they oppose such a dilution of the IE technology?

The status of IE may be inferred from the categories of sources, which include answers from interviews with headmasters, IE teachers, other teachers and parents, and the results of the primary school examination which is required for entrance to the IE schools. Both sources demonstrate that IE is highly valued as a secondary school subject. Whether or not this is directly related to the project's content is not easily determined.

7.5 Evaluation of the logistical components

Industrial Education requires rather complicated and costly logistics to suit its needs: workshops, equipment, tools, materials, consumables, plus often extensive repair and maintenance. It is not unusual for the costs of equipment and tools to greatly exceed the cost of the building structure that houses them. Some general areas that were considered by the evaluation team as regards logistics will be outlined below, along with comments on the manner in which the evaluating team assessed them.

How fully was the workshop capacity utilized?

Table 9. Utilization of workshop capacity

	\multicolumn{7}{c}{Utilization of school IE capacity}
	For one student. No. of weekly IE periods for a 4-year course	No. of students in Form IV	\multicolumn{2}{c}{Student periods per week (no. of students x no. of periods)}	\multicolumn{2}{c}{Teaching periods per week}	Average class size per teaching period
			In the workshop	Total no. of periods	In the workshop	Total no. of periods	
School	(1)	(2)	(3)	(4)	(5)	(6)	(7)
(Official target for a three-stream school)	(24)	(40)	(1280)	(1920)	(64)	(84)	(23)

Source: Lauglo (1985:95).

The Evaluation Study of Industrial Education in Kenya

The evaluation team investigated how fully the workshop capacity was utilized in any given year in relation to the number of IE students. The utilization of school IE capacity was assessed by comparing the official target with the figures gathered from each school. An adaptation from the Kenyan assessment is presented in Table 9. By assembling a chart such as this, and figuring out the official targets beforehand, one can more easily specify and search out the necessary data.

Money spent on IE materials - was it spent on IE?

In Section 7.7 we shall consider costs in greater detail. Here, however, it may be useful to comment on the assessment of the financing of the logistical components. At various levels from the government down to the school, finances were earmarked for IE, and clearly this money should be spent on the costs of IE. In assessing this aspect the former Swedish teachers, the headmasters and the Kenyan IE teachers were asked specific questions. In the tracer study, the Swedish teachers were asked, for example, "Were there any serious problems in being able to actually use money earmarked for IE? If so, how were such problems solved?" The headmasters were asked, "What difficulties do you, as a headmaster, experience in having IE at your school?" Finally, two examples of the questions put before the IE teachers concerning IE finances were, "Exactly how much money do you have to run the IE workshop?" And, "In general, how difficult is it for you to get the money so that it can be spent on IE?"

The condition of workshops and equipment

An observation schedule was used during the visits to schools in order to assess the condition of workshops and equipment. This was supplemented by questions to the IE teachers. In the observation schedule, a number of items were rated on a 5-point scale:

Very poor / Poor / Fair / Good / Very good

The quality of the workshops and their equipment was checked in 39 out of 69 workshops (most schools had 2 workshops). The observation schedule considered the following aspects: (a) the condition of the workshop buildings and the workshop organization and planning; (b) workshop tools and equipment care, repair and maintenance; and (c) teaching and learning resources (Nyagah, 1985).

The role of the maintenance unit

Questions were put to the IE teachers concerning the role of the Maintenance Unit, both in their individual questionnaires and in group interviews. A few examples of these questions include:

> "When were you last visited by the Maintenance Unit personnel?"
> "What, if any, improvements are needed in the services of the Maintenance Unit?"
> "Do you regularly buy materials from the Maintenance Unit?"

Was the IE equipment too advanced?

In assessing this area, questions were asked of the former Swedish teachers, the headmasters and the IE teachers. Examples of the questions for each group are listed below.

```
Former Swedish IE teachers
```

> "Looking back, do you see any serious mistakes in the way IE was developed in Kenya? Are there any lessons for its future development in Kenyan schools?"
> "If IE were to be introduced in most schools, how would the subject need to be changed, if at all?"

```
Kenyan Headmasters and IE Teachers
```

> "What mistakes were made in the way IE was developed as a subject in the country as a whole?"
> "How would IE need to be changed if it is to be offered in many more secondary schools?"

These questions, and this area as a whole, were developed and probed in the group interviews with the IE teachers. It should be noted also that a photographic survey of the IE workshops was conducted. This survey provided a qualitative indicator of the quality and condition of the logistical components which complemented other measures.

7.6 Evaluation of the personnel components

The teachers were the only category of personnel subjected to the evaluation study. However, the opinions and attitudes of the headmasters were used not only as indicators of the teacher performance and the status of IE, but also as an indication of their role in the schools. Concerning the IE teachers and their teaching practices, six areas were chosen for investigation. Below we shall briefly highlight these areas and comment on the manner in which they were assessed.

Characteristics of the IE teachers. In order to identify the characteristics of the teachers, items on the questionnaire probed various aspects in order to reveal: (a) their educational qualifications; (b) the amount of practical work experience they had which related to the practical skills taught; and (c) how much teaching experience they had.

Professional morale. IE teachers participated in both group interviews and questionnaires. Concerning professional morale, the IE teachers, the headmasters and "other teachers" were asked such questions as:

"Actual teaching time is only a part of the teacher's work. How much extra time do you think is needed in IE as compared with academic subjects in order to prepare, maintain equipment, etc.?"

"In your case, are you happy with the balance in your present teaching load between IE and your academic subject?"

"How satisfied are you with being a teacher?"

"If you could start your life all over again, what occupation would you most like to have?"

"Do you think that you will be teaching in ten years' time?"

The compiled answers to these questions were compared between the different groups of respondents. From these compilations it appeared that the "other teachers" were more committed to their jobs. Additionally, all of the groups of respondents agreed that IE was more demanding and time-consuming than the academic subjects

Perceived competence of IE teachers. Twenty of 34 headmasters were interviewed at length, and an impression was made upon the evaluator of good rapport and authenticity of answers. Concerning the perceived competence of the IE teachers, the headmasters were asked to compare and rate the IE teachers with the "other teachers". The scale they were to rate them on was as follows:

| Better / Slightly better / About the same / Slightly worse / Worse |

As many of the IE teachers were also qualified to teach an academic subject, the headmasters were asked, "Are the IE teachers in general better at teaching IE, or are they better at teaching their academic subject?"

Comparing Swedish volunteers and Kenyan teachers. In assessing this area, items were included in the tracer survey of the former Swedish volunteers, and in the questionnaires of IE teachers and headmasters. Below are a few of the relevant questions examined in assessing this area.

> **From the tracer study of former Swedish teachers**

"At your school(s), how far had the workshops been established and equipped by the time you arrived?"
"What are the strengths and weaknesses of trained Kenyan IE teachers as compared with Swedish volunteer teachers?"

> **From the IE teachers' and headmasters' questionnaire**

"In your opinion were the Swedish teachers less able, about the same, or more able than most Kenyan IE teachers in each of the following areas: (1) communicating in English; (2) establishing workshops; (3) teaching IE theory; (4) teaching IE practicals; (5) maintenance and repair?"

The questionnaire sent to all 45 Swedish volunteer teachers who worked in the project during its first phase was successfully completed and returned by 85 per cent of them. They were asked to give their opinion on, among other things, the status and position of IE and their understanding of the official aims of IE. The majority of them said that they perceived IE as a blend between general and pre-vocational education. Overall, they did not believe that IE had a great influence on the students' search for work and they were of the opinion that the equipment in the workshops was too advanced for its purpose.

How did they teach the practical aspect of IE? The practical aspect of IE was heavily emphasized in the IE objectives. IE was intended to develop creativity, initiative and problem-solving abilities, using an applied workshop approach. However, these are rather difficult items to identify and measure. For the most part, the evaluation team utilized the group interviews of IE teachers to find the relevant information. Some other examples of measures used to assess the practical aspect of IE are given below.

The time allocated to practical work done in the workshops was compared with the recommended time allocation, which was four of the six 40-minute periods per week. One of the evaluators collected data from 14 schools offering wood/metalwork courses and 5 offering mechanics/electrical courses. The period allocated for practical lessons was studied and observations were made in the workshops and classrooms. The time allocation of time varied somewhat between schools, but in general, less time than recommended was spent on activities in the workshops.

The relationship that existed between the theoretical and practical activities (see 4.4) was also assessed from school visits. One of the evaluators carried out a survey in 12 schools of the practical projects made by the students. With help from the teachers, all the projects made were classified according to the degree of freedom the students were given in design. There was a scale of four classifications which ranged from a situation where all the students made the same project according to the same design, to a situation where total freedom was allowed to the students both in terms of the task and in the design.

Teachers' views of exams and syllabuses. In assessing this final aspect regarding the IE teachers, the group interviews of IE teachers (and questionnaires from the IE teachers who did not participate in group interviews) provided the means to obtain the necessary information. Two examples of the questions asked were:

"Some people think that the IE syllabuses are too detailed so what teachers have too little choice in what to teach. What do you think?"

"How satisfied are you with the way IE is examined?"

In addition, IE exam results from different schools were compared in order to note any changes or alternations in scores between schools and in relation to the controlling scores in the academic subject exams.

7.7 Evaluation of the project performance

One very important element of project performance is the evaluation of costs. In this evaluation, costs were restricted to government and student (fee) expenditures. This reflected one of the general aims of the evaluation, which was to illustrate donor and government decision-making. Also, such indirect expenditures as earnings foregone were not included because of the difficulty in locating reliable primary sources--this area was also not one of the focuses of the evaluation. Overall, the evaluation considered expenditures by the Government of Kenya and SIDA, as well as school fees. Unfortunately, data on all expenditures were not available in all schools. The following costs were estimated: recurrent expenditures; capital expenditures; subject costs; costs per student, student period and class; relative teaching costs, i.e. cost per teacher period; and comparative costs of institutions.

In Chapter 4, we pointed out the need to structure cost estimates to include both capital and recurrent costs. We also suggested a basic scheme to outline the basic types of data necessary. The Kenyan IE evaluation basically followed the suggested steps mentioned in Chapter 4. Both capital and recurrent expenditures were estimated, organized and later compared between subjects and schools, and even to a small degree between different years--as data allowed. Estimates on recurrent expenditures were obtained from 23 out of the 35 included schools. The source for this information came from records of the Ministry of Education. Next the unit recurrent cost, or the expenditures per student, was figured and these data could then be compared with other institutions.

In figuring capital expenditures, SIDA project files were used as the main source of data. This was particularly necessary because after the completion of the KS Industrial Education Project in 1981, there was little spent on capital expenditures by the Kenyan Government. The capital costs, here, refer basically to the buildings, infrastructure (staff housing) and equipment for the workshops. The costs, in most cases, were converted to 1981 prices. In estimating per place per year costs, a life of twenty years was assumed for the buildings and ten years for the equipment. The subject costs were also figured in the evaluation which allowed comparison between the IE subjects and the academic subjects. Basically, subject cost can be estimated in the following manner (see Lauglo, 1985:138):

> Subject costs = teaching costs of each subject + consumable/recurrent expenditures + yearly costs of the capital + share of the overheads including administration

Of course, it would not be proper to compare total subject costs because enrolments and period allocation may vary greatly between subjects and between schools. Thus, this total subject cost should be broken down to cost per student, per student period or per class period, as was done in the Kenyan IE evaluation. It was found that IE was on all indicators more expensive than other subjects, due mainly to the workshops and their expensive equipment, and the lower ratio of students to teachers in the workshops. This, of course, is typical for technical/vocational education.

The long-term effects, outcomes and impact of IE are very important when considering project performance. In the IE evaluation, the following studies were made in order to estimate the long-term effects, outcomes and impact of IE in Kenya:
1. A long-term tracer study (retrospective) ten years back. The 14 ex-students of the first IE class that completed their education in 1974 were interviewed. They were asked to describe their plans, aspirations, ambitions, and so on, just before and after they left school. They also answered questions concerning the use of their IE knowledge.
2. Interviews with 1,600 students in Form IV in 15 IE schools in 1983. Next, there was another follow-up study of these students one year after the examination. A new follow-up of the same students three years after their examination was later completed. Many of the questions concerning career and attitudes were open-ended and the classification of the answers was made afterwards. The ex-students were asked to mention what kind of work they would like if they could choose freely, and what kind of work they actually expected to find. The low response rate to the follow-up evaluations demonstrated one of the difficulties with evaluation studies (particularly tracer studies) in developing countries, and furthermore this low response rate makes conclusions risky.

3. A tracer study in 3 schools. The ex-students had a questionnaire sent to them one year after their examination. The results here more or less confirmed and better illustrated the results of the other studies.
4. A small-scale survey of employers in Nairobi and its environs. Thirteen employers with a staff from 95 to 5,000 were selected in Nairobi and its environs. It appears that they were selected because former IE students were employed there (according to the teachers).

In concluding this section and chapter, it may be useful to look at the aims of the evaluation (which are rather general) and the methods, indicators and sources that the evaluation team utilized in pursuing these aims.

1. *To identify the aims and objectives of IE in Kenya, to examine these in the Kenyan and international contexts and to trace the main influences on the evolution of aims, objectives and syllabuses.*

The historical background and the influences upon these objectives were traced through documents concerning secondary education and vocational education in the United Kingdom, Sweden and Kenya. The evaluation team was able to illustrate the influence from the former colonial power as well as that from the aid donors (Canada and Sweden) that were directly involved in the vocationalization of secondary education in Kenya.

2. *To assess the degree of success of IE both in terms of its official objectives and in terms of the expectations which are held by students, teachers, headmasters, parents and employers. Also, to identify unanticipated outcomes of IE.*

The principal methods and sources here were the surveys and tracer studies. First, the official objectives (and the degree of compatibility/incompatibility between them) were analysed. This was done with the help of official Kenyan documents. Then the operation and outcomes of the project were investigated through the surveys and tracer studies. These studies also provided information about the expectations of the various groups of people mentioned.

3. *To identify the conditions which have influenced the degree of success of IE, and to identify the main difficulties or problems pertaining to it, as perceived by those involved in implementing IE or by those directly affected by IE subjects.*

The first of these issues was not very clearly operationalized. This applies in particular to the phrase, "conditions which have influenced". The perceptions held by those involved were investigated in surveys and interviews.

4. *To examine the cost of IE as compared with other parts of general secondary education and with vocational training.*

Various measures and indicators were used and the sources came from existing documents in the schools. It was possible to establish valid, reliable measures for the comparisons.

5. *To assess the future role of IE in the schools, within the framework of present educational policy in Kenya.*

On the basis of interviews and participant observations in the schools, content analysis of educational documents and cost analysis, the team was able to make the recommendation that IE in its present form could not be extended to a large number of schools. It was too expensive to be extended and the education was too specialized in relation to the labour-market needs.

6. *To assess Swedish aid to IE in the light of the general aims for SIDA's work and to suggest guidelines for SIDA with respect to possible future involvement with similar curriculum change in other countries.*

The localization of the schools in the project and their recruitment of students, as well as the performance of the project, were analysed mainly with the help of surveys (and tracer studies) and the findings were compared to the SIDA objectives.

Conclusions and major recommendations

General conclusions

Many notions of how evaluations should be carried out and how they can be more efficacious became apparent from the content of Part One. In the discussion of the role and nature of educational evaluation, it is important to emphasize the continuity aspect developed in Chapter 1. Ideally, educational evaluation should be part and parcel of all phases or stages of an educational plan, policy, programme or project. It should be neither only summative "product-oriented" nor only formative "process-oriented", but should instead include both complementary dimensions. It is equally important to re-evaluate the role of educational evaluation *vis-à-vis* its contribution to the cost-reduction and cost-effectiveness of programmes and projects. Evaluation should not merely be the "watch-dog" in providing information for those concerned about whether or not the programme or project has achieved its objectives, but instead it should be considered as a "participant", living with and monitoring achievements and shortcomings of the said programme or project.

Evaluation should pay greater attention to organizational issues, as crude measures of inputs and outputs do not always accommodate the major determinants of success or failure of an educational or social intervention programme. Here, leadership style, programme staff's behaviour and attitudes, participation of the clientele, information and communication linkages, and so on, constitute a vital body of information to be gathered for good-quality evaluation. There are many different types of evaluation models and strategies; each bears given evaluation functions and the choice among them should depend upon the nature and quality of the educational programme or project under evaluation. Unfortunately, only a few models use a holistic approach to educational evaluation (comprehensive and systematic evaluation model). They often either focus on process evaluation (e.g. classroom observation) or on impact evaluation (e.g. experimental curriculum).

It is important to note that most debates concerning the role and purpose of evaluation do not consider the evaluatees, yet this element should not be overlooked. Educational programmes and projects are usually very complex in nature and are generally addressed to heterogeneous clientele with distinct and conflicting interests, needs, values and expectations. These dimensions should be carefully considered in any evaluational endeavour. Too much emphasis has been previously given to technico-rational aspects of educational evaluation using macro-economic and mathematical models. The human dimensions have been underestimated or deliberately left out. None the less, there is today greater concern and interest in re-evaluating the experiences from the "other sciences" before their application and use in the field of educational evaluation.

After considering some of the major operational issues in educational evaluation, it becomes quite obvious that information in particular is an area deserving much greater attention in educational evaluation. In this field, a solid platform should be ensured to maintain the linkages between information, co-ordination and communication. These linkages are pertinent to the many users of evaluation activities as they have different perceptions of the use of evaluation. Therefore, the success of utilization-focused evaluations depends upon the nature of the linkages between information, co-ordination and communication, and on the abilities of the evaluator to facilitate the involvement of the different groups concerned. These considerations are imperative for educational evaluation as they affect the utility of evaluation with respect to relevance, communication between evaluator and user, the manner of information processing employed by users, the credibility of the evaluation and the level of involvement of the potential users. Questions about the depth and breadth of the information base should be treated from the standpoint of the complementary role of quantitative and qualitative evaluation designs and paradigms.

The designing of the evaluation and the choice of techniques and instruments to be used should be done carefully and stringently. There are several elements of design, such as sampling, matching and control groups, that need to be considered. The choice of evaluation design or designs should not be divorced from the choice of indicators and variables for evaluation as, unfortunately, is often the case. Sometimes, a significant amount of information already available from other sources is collected while some pertinent types of information are left out. The choice of indicators and variables should therefore be built-in to the evaluation design or designs. The data collected should reflect, in the first place, the purpose and objectives of the evaluation. It should be made clear right from the beginning of the evaluation which analytical strategy is espoused and how such a strategy corresponds to the information needs of the targeted evaluation audience.

Quality educational evaluation cannot be ensured without a holistic approach to education and to educational evaluation. This demands a proper understanding of the interplay among frame factors and their components (see Figure 3).

Attention to the relevant principles and practices in educational evaluation should be paramount. As developed in Part Two, the knowledge and experience of evaluations within differing areas of education can be both complementary and overlapping. Some of the more common overall aspects to be considered in evaluating educational programmes and projects include: (a) organizational and administrative setting of programmes and projects; (b) budgetary allocation and ceilings; (c) programme coverage (the target clientele); (d) logistics (availability of physical, material and human resources; (e) information-dissemination systems; and (f) desired outputs.

It is important to note that in most education systems, the common aims and objectives of primary education are to provide: (a) basic knowledge and skills; (b) an overall education and development of children; and (c) a foundation for subsequent education. None the less, country-specific aims and objectives for primary education should be properly examined in an educational evaluation. Equally important for the evaluation of primary education is a retrospective analysis of these aims and objectives over a longer time-period. Some principal areas where determined efforts need to be ensured in order to ascertain good-quality primary education evaluation include: (a) policy analysis; (b) evaluation design; (c) theory and model-building; (d) pre-planning of evaluation - pre-testing and pilot studies; (e) instrument construction and development; (f) methods and techniques; and (g) participatory evaluation.

The aims and objectives of literacy programmes and campaigns also need to be carefully explored. The country-specific contexts together with the programme-specific contexts should be properly understood before, and in the course of, evaluation. Furthermore, serious consideration should be given to the scope and coverage of literacy programmes where important domains are often not captured in conventional educational evaluations, for example, the contribution of literacy to health, nutrition, fertility and productivity. Relevant elements of literacy programmes such as programme setting, finances, the learners, the instructors, instructional materials, teaching, logistics, mass media contributions and outputs need to be weighed in order to direct and facilitate the evaluation activities. In addition, the evaluation objectives themselves need to be considered, and distinctions made between immediate and long-term objectives. Similar distinctions need to be made between the measurable outcomes, as well as the unmeasurable and unexpected outcomes of literacy programmes when they are evaluated. In addition, other sources of data on literacy programmes should be explored to avoid the evaluator's and evaluatee's burden in dealing with long questionnaires, lengthy interviews, and so on.

Scope, domain and depth of vocational/technical programmes are important elements of educational evaluation. Once the programme setting is considered, the evaluation setting including designs, paradigms and methodologies comes into focus. For example, the evaluation may have to treat many subsystems of technical/vocational education (the decision-making and management subsystem, the teacher corps subsystem, the curriculum subsystem, the logistics subsystem, the selected students subsystem, etc.). These subsystems have to be studied in relation to each other and to the objectives set for technical/vocational education in general. Besides relating the objectives of technical/vocational education to the operational linkages among these subsystems, evaluation should also focus on the linkages between input, process and output indicators. Some of these indicators were mentioned in Chapter 4. Evaluation of technical/vocational education programmes is a difficult and complex exercise. Over and above the points mentioned earlier, it is imperative to consider all the components of the programmes in an evaluation, i.e. programme content, logistics and personnel, in order to arrive at an accurate, justifiable and objective evaluation of the programmes' performance.

Practical experiences in educational evaluation are not always recorded in detail as people are often not interested in the process of planning and conducting an educational evaluation; instead the emphasis is given to the outcomes of the evaluation. Yet, especially in the context of developing countries, the practical experiences are of utmost importance and yet have been largely overlooked in the literature dealing with evaluation. It was our intention in this book to address this topic in particular and in Part Three we presented and assessed three evaluation experiences from developing countries.

The patterns and directions of influence and growth within educational evaluation largely preclude the developing countries. The comprehensive approach to educational evaluation explains our perception of evaluation as a discipline that is interlinked between the problematic issues, the strategic concerns and the pragmatic experiences of educational evaluation. But the patterns that are well established mirror the issues and experiences of the North. In better establishing the patterns of our approach to reflect the South, much needs to be done to strengthen and develop the research capacity in developing countries. Along with this, the means of information dissemination will need to be established and developed in order to influence the discipline and help it grow and better include the interests of the developing countries. In this next and final section we present and discuss some overall recommendations that should prove fruitful in the discussion and resolution of evaluation difficulties experienced in the Third World.

Building evaluation capacity in developing countries

The condition and status of educational evaluation in the developing countries are in important respects different from the industrialized North, just as the conditions and milieu of their educational programmes and projects are different. As a whole, the developing countries are financially constrained by their increasing debts and their creditors' pressure to alter their economies towards more conducive structures of exploitation. This often results in further cuts in the social sector and a further dependence on external agencies to support social interventions and their evaluations.

Like the industrial revolution, and the major technical and structural changes that followed, evaluation was initiated and has flourished in North America and Europe, only later appearing in the largely non-industrialized South. And like the industrialization process, evaluation has been steered South and largely managed by the North. Thus educational evaluation in the developing countries has largely been built upon the theory and methods developed in the North. While the borrowed and adapted structures and techniques have proved helpful and rewarding, they are often off target and not as adequate as their conditions might require.

There are, however, many inherent problems in the research climate of the developing countries. For example, one reason for the slow progress of evaluation in the developing countries is the under-utilization of existing research and evaluation experience in these countries themselves. Below we shall reflect upon some experiences of evaluating educational programmes in developing countries, including the three evaluations considered in Chapters 5, 6 and 7. An overview of needs, obstacles and prospects will be presented and discussed according to three major areas of concern for educational evaluation in these countries: (a) climate for educational evaluation; (b) strategies for South-South co-operation; and (c) modalities for capacity-building.

Climate for educational evaluation

The climate of evaluation and research work largely determines its success and appropriate utilization. In referring to climate, we consider the political, economic and socio-cultural backdrop as well as the institutional setting in which the evaluative work is conducted. Evaluation, when confined to programmes of social intervention, and to education in particular, must be properly designed, opportunely organized and effectively implemented. This should be especially the case in developing countries where resources are relatively more scarce. In many of these countries, problems arise in relation to the contexts and processes of building educational evaluation, research and training capacities. In others, educational evaluation is still an unrecognized and a non-organized scientific pursuit often characterized by piecemeal approaches and efforts.

Two of the most recent comprehensive reviews of the environments of educational evaluation and research in developing countries (Shaeffer and Nkinyangi, 1983; Gopinathan and Nielson, 1988) have emphasized that a tolerant and supportive climate is a prerequisite for effective generation and conduct of good-quality evaluation and research. Although there are increasingly concerted efforts among policy-makers, programme administrators, front-line implementors and target beneficiaries to institutionalize educational evaluation, the support has so far been minimal. A great deal of the innovation and improvement in educational evaluation still remains a by-product of the works of scholars and researchers in the developed and affluent nations. Lacunae in the field of educational evaluation in developing countries are partly due to the poor capacity to examine critically the progress achieved elsewhere in the field with a view to building up the evaluation capacity tailored to specific contexts, needs and aspirations. Instead, the choice is often that of espousing evaluation models, approaches, designs, instruments, and so on that have been developed in the industrialized countries and are often considered to be the most legitimate or easiest route. Wu Wei (1986:29) cautions against this in the case of China: "In studying foreign educational theories and experience, we must adhere to the principle of 'making foreign things serve China' and proceeding from China's actual conditions, paying attention to what can be or cannot be compared between China and foreign countries."

Nevertheless, evaluation is becoming ever more commonplace in the developing countries where its impact is being felt. Unfortunately, modern evaluation in the South is less efficacious than evaluation in the North. The infrastructure of many developing countries is not sufficiently developed to make evaluation an easy and viable task. This infrastructure is related not only to the communication links, but also to the overall research capacity which is built upon education, specialized training and information processing, storage and dissemination. There are many major constraints on building educational evaluation capacity in developing countries, including: (a) a perception that educational evaluation is still largely unrecognized and unorganized as a scientific pursuit; (b) piecemeal approaches, individual efforts and initiatives according to the "contract-contact principle"; (c) largely unpublished research and evaluation experience; (d) overall poor-quality evaluation; and (e) dependence upon foreign expertise and funds. This then results in further cuts in the social sector and a further dependence on external agencies to support social intervention programmes and their evaluations.

In addition, barriers need to be breached between countries in the South where information is often not properly disseminated. In the case of South-East Asia, the most serious problem in the evaluation and research environments concerns the utilization of research findings (Gopinathan and Nielson, 1988). These authors consider that the most obvious solution to this is to improve the communication and interaction among researchers within the region. Yet such claims are not new. In his review of educational research and training in the Indian Ocean states of eastern and southern Africa, Chinapah (1986) observes that due to academic competition and inter- and intra-institutional barriers, there are severe constraints on the generation and promotion of good-quality educational evaluation in these countries. Very little is done to promote capacity-building programmes in educational evaluation and research at departmental or institutional levels.

One of the major difficulties in the implementation of educational policies in developing countries is the treatment and management of conflicting goals and conflicting interest groups. In both situations, evaluation and monitoring exercises become more demanding but fruitful. Burnham (1973) argues for a theoretical framework with "controlled" conflict where pluralism, disagreement and partial consensus are accommodated. Chinapah and Fägerlind (1986:6) argue that the institutionalization of conflict from the standpoint of educational evaluation calls for the following:
1. A participatory system of evaluation where implementors, evaluators, monitors and the actual beneficiaries (school administrators, teachers, community leaders, parents and students) may examine critically in a forum sensitive policy issues or policy options in order to manage conflict.
2. An information-dissemination system of evaluation where there are flows of information bottom-up and top-down at both vertical and horizontal levels of educational administration and management.
3. A political climate for evaluation that enables self-criticism, inter- as well as intra-administrative and departmental disagreement and critiques and positive discriminatory measures to the advantage of the weakest without any damage or harm to specific individuals, groups or institutional bodies.

In developing countries, evaluations and evaluators must deal with several constraints in the course of their work. Occasionally, problems in evaluation arise as a result of resistance, or the lack of willingness to co-operate on the part of managers and other "stakeholders". This friction may occur because the stakeholders cannot grasp the purpose of the evaluation or because of self-interest. It is often argued that the problems of implementing educational programmes do not arise from the technical-rational arena, but are rooted in the socio-economic and political arenas. Yet another difficulty with the evaluation of educational programmes is that the evaluation results are simply not used to improve and adapt the programmes they were intended for. Such a situation was experienced in conducting evaluations of eleven different projects in the Experimental World Literacy Programme (EWLP) in developing countries (Spaulding, 1985).

Evaluation of educational programmes in the developing countries is viewed differently by the different actors involved. For example, donor agencies are more likely to use evaluations for future planning and the setting of priorities, while national administrators and programme implementors seem to be more interested in evaluation information to help improve programme efficiency and effectiveness. Poor dissemination is further complicated by the often obvious under-utilization of the research by policy-makers. This situation often occurs even in the industrialized countries (see Husén and Kogan, 1984).

The work and achievements of evaluators and researchers in the southern hemisphere are underrepresented in established journals and in scholarly debates. This may partly explain the underestimation and underrating of their knowledge by those who are planning and implementing evaluation in these countries. Likewise, there are several questions and problems that arise with the extensive training of people from the South in the North. In their review of the environments of educational research in South-East Asian countries, Gopinathan and Nielson (1988) observe that the training and preparation received in the North often mean that researchers from the South are incapable of reconciling their training with their indigenous evaluation and research climate. Much remains to be done to improve the climate for educational evaluation in developing countries.

Strategies for South-South co-operation

More attention needs to be paid to, and use made of, the already existing evaluation experience in the developing countries. In considering concrete practical experiences we can come to understand better not only the lacunae in educational evaluation in developing countries but also the difficult conditions under which evaluation has to operate. From such experiences, the importance of capacity-building in educational evaluation becomes ever more apparent. While it is appropriate and revealing to consider the centre-periphery relationship in educational evaluation, there is also a need to realize the overall interdependence between the North and the South in this field. Much needs to be done and what has been done is not always conducive to the needs and expectations of countries in both the North and South. It is true that some aspects of contemporary educational evaluation designs, methods and instruments are relevant to the evaluation of programmes and projects in developing countries, but in the course of their implementation, other more important issues need to be considered.

Shaeffer and Nkinyangi (1983) advocate flexibility in training as one approach for the developing nations to satisfy better their own needs for educational evaluation and research. This means not only increasing the number of researchers, but also seeing to it that there is a greater mix of their skills. They also recommend a greater flexibility and imagination in the climate for evaluation and research. The problem of regional capacity-building is often inherent in the notion that quality programming can only be available in the industrialized North. The tendency to focus on the development of national capacity for educational evaluation for people from developing countries deserves considerable attention. For example, in the three reviews of the environments of educational evaluation and research in developing countries (Shaeffer and Nkinyangi, 1983; Chinapah, 1986; Gopinathan and Nielson, 1988) it is clear that very little is done at national and regional levels in the South to promote and facilitate research and training programmes in educational evaluation and research.

South-South co-operation in educational evaluation is still in its infancy. For example, joint evaluation and research ventures are seldom carried out, partly because of the shortage of resources and partly because of the poor climate to generate, conduct and perform joint evaluation ventures. Developing regional training capacity can also be thwarted by financial arrangements from donor agencies, foreign governments and universities for training at the universities in the developed countries. However, the indigenous and regional training programmes initiated have so far received prompt support and encouragement from the major donor agencies who see this as more cost-efficient in the short run and more effective in the long run. Regional programmes for training of trainers are a case in point. At both regional and national levels, such programmes are designed to bring about the so-called multiplier effects in the area of capacity-building in educational evaluation and research.

Modalities for capacity-building

Joint evaluation and research ventures need to be undertaken to fill the existing gaps in applicable information and the many common themes prevalent in the context of educational evaluation in developing countries. Issues to be addressed might include linguistic and language problems, equality of educational opportunity, curriculum relevance and innovation, cost-effectiveness, education and employment, and educational reforms. Efforts to create documentation centres for indigenous research and evaluation experience would also prove constructive. While education in the developing countries continues to undergo extensive growth and reform, educational research and evaluation dealing with the reform process, the assessment of pilot programmes or innovations and/or the comparison of new and existing educational schemes remains most urgent and useful.

Funding patterns also need to be examined. Here the problem is not a purely economic one, but is also a result of the presence of many funding agencies (bilateral and multilateral) with various aims and objectives. The funding of educational evaluation and research has to be thoroughly considered in order to avoid problems of wastage of scarce resources, duplication of evaluation and research work, creation of unnecessary infrastructures and the design of inappropriate evaluation programmes and projects that increase the dependence upon the North, while not contributing to the general research competence and capacity in the particular countries where these evaluations are carried out.

Some developing countries have established "centres of excellence" for promoting regional capacity-building in educational evaluation and research. To reduce the heavy dependence for capacity-building in educational evaluation and research upon universities and tertiary institutions in North America and Europe, these centres could be supported for regional capacity-building programmes. Such a modality could be used for graduate-research training or for recruitment of educational researchers among the research institutions of countries in the region. Research and training gaps in the region can be decreased by regional courses in educational and other related sciences at certificate, diploma or degree level. In other words, the regional infrastructures need to be utilized in the promotion of staff development programmes and educational evaluation and research capacity-building for the advancement of potential knowledge, skills and competence that can be shared by individuals, departments and institutions in these countries. Possibilities for such activities are many and include, for example, short-term courses or workshops in educational research methodology.

Regional short-term intensive training courses and workshops can enrich the educational evaluation and research capacity of these countries and serve as a platform for the identification of common educational evaluation and research problems and issues, or for the setting up of joint educational research ventures. The regional contexts of these countries offer a wide range of possibilities to study common educational evaluation and research themes. In the area of information, documentation and dissemination of educational evaluation and research results, similar possibilities and gaps exist; regional co-operation can be highly beneficial and useful in the process of reinforcing the existing capacity. In a similar vein, regional educational evaluation and research are often not well disseminated in journals or newsletters to highlight the present co-operation and experience, as well as to point out further needs, gaps and constraints in the field.

While in some regions institutions and networks have initiated or are planning to initiate regional training programmes, they are still largely under-utilized (Chinapah, 1988). In view of the acute shortage of and increasing need for regional evaluation and research training programmes, the following recommendations have been made:

1. The promotion of regional evaluation and research training programmes at certificate, diploma and degree level in education and educational-related sciences.
2. The development of short courses, seminars and workshops in educational evaluation and research methodology.
3. The maintenance of a permanent infrastructure for exchange of evaluation and research training personnel (teachers/researchers) among the regional institutions.
4. The provision of facilities for pre-training and in-service training of teacher trainers in educational evaluation and research in the respective regions.

At the national level, capacity-building in educational evaluation requires an improvement of the existing infrastructures in most developing countries. This should include the following: (a) staff development programmes for educational evaluators and researchers as well as their support personnel; (b) creation and/or improvement of documentation, publication and storage facilities; and (c) assistance for information and dissemination of evaluation and research works.

Knowledge is said to be universal. The same could be said of the available stock of evaluation methods, techniques and experiences accumulated in the North. Advocating indigenous educational evaluation and research does not necessarily mean disregarding the knowledge available. Yet a problem often arises in the interpretation of the experiences accrued in the North and in the application of the methods and techniques utilized in drastically different climates. Most approaches, designs, methods and techniques are universally applicable; however, adjustments and adaptations must be made from country to country and from context to context. While the problems and suggestions pointed out here are generally recognized, more effort and action are needed in the developing countries to promote and improve their national capacity for educational evaluation and research in order to meet their present needs and future demands.

What needs to be done and what we are suggesting is enormous. And while we - like so many others - hope to effect positive change and provide some answers or solutions, we are cognizant that educational evaluation is only a small link in the advancement of education and the people it affects, just as it is a small factor in the larger socio-economic-political milieu. There are many directions and paths that the developing countries might take in their quest for more effective and appropriate means of evaluation and planning. A more productive and viable path is becoming apparent as a result of better co-operation and, in particular, a better understanding of the practical experiences and genuine conditions and obstacles present in the Third World context. This is where we intend, and hope, that this book will make a contribution.

Bibliography

Academy of Educational Planning and Management. 1984. *Pre-Service Training Programme in Educational Planning and Management.* Islamabad, AEPM.
Alexander, L.; Simmons, J. 1975. The Determinants of School Achievement in Developing Countries: The Education Production Function Model. *World Bank Staff Working Paper, No. 201.* Washington, D.C., World Bank.
Alkin, M.; Ellett, J. 1985. Evaluation Models: Development. In: T. Husén and T. Postlethwaite (eds.), *The International Encyclopedia of Education,* Vol. 3, pp. 1760-6. Oxford, Pergamon Press.
Babbie, E. 1973. *Survey Research Methods.* Calif., Wadsworth.
Bacchus, K. 1988. The Political Context of Vocationalization of Education. In: J. Lauglo and K. Lillis (eds.) *Vocationalizing Education: An International Perspective.* Oxford, Pergamon Press.
Benson, J.; Michael, W. 1987. Designing Evaluation Studies: A Twenty-year Perspective. *International Journal of Educational Research,* 11(1):43-56.
Berk, R.; Rossi, P. 1976. Doing Well or Worse: Evaluation Research Politically Reexamined. *Social Problems,* 23(2):337-49.
Bhola, H. 1979. *Evaluating Functional Literacy,* Literacy in Development: A Series of Training Monographs. Tehran, International Institute for Adult Literacy Methods.
Bloom, B. 1964. *Stability and Change in Human Characteristics.* New York, John Wiley & Sons.
Bohrnstedt, G. 1969. Observations on the Measurement of Change. In: E. Borgatta (ed.), *Sociological Methodology,* 113-33. San Francisco, Calif., Jossey-Bass.
Boudhiba, A. 1980. The Universal and the Particular in Educational Goals. In: Unesco, *Educational Goals.* Paris, Unesco-IBE. (Studies and Surveys in Comparative Education.)
Bowles, S. 1968. *Towards an Educational Production Function.* A Paper prepared for the Conference on Research in Income and Wealth. Madison, Wis. (Mimeo.)
Bowman, M. 1988. Links between General and Vocational Education: Does the One Enhance the Other? *International Review of Education,* 34(2).
Burnham, R. A. 1973. Systems Evaluation and Goal Disagreement. In: E.R. House (ed.), *School Evaluation: The Politics and Process.* Berkeley, Calif. McCutchan Publishing Corporation.
Carron, G.; Chau, T. (eds.). 1981. *Reducing of Regional Disparities: The Role of Educational Planning.* Paris, Unesco-IIEP.
CERID (Centre for Educational Research, Innovation and Development). 1985. *School Level Curriculum: A Historical Perspective.* Sano Thimi, (Nepal), Education Press J.E.M.C.
Chinapah, V. 1983a. Participation and Performance in Primary Schooling. *Studies in Comparative and International Education, No.8.* Stockholm, Institute of International Education, University of Stockholm.
——. 1983b. The Mauritian National Survey: A Presentation of Instruments and Manuals. *Working Paper Series No. 56,* Stockholm, Institute of International Education, University of Stockholm.
——. 1984. *The Ethiopian Literacy Campaign Evaluation.* Ottawa, International Development Research Centre (IDRC).
——. 1986. *Educational Research and Training in the Indian Ocean States of Eastern and Southern African Region - Mauritius, Madagascar and Seychelles.* Ottawa, International Development Research Centre (IDRC).
——. 1988. *Regional Technical Cooperation in Education for Human Resources Development in Africa.* Dakar,(Senegal), Unesco Regional Office for Education in Africa.
Chinapah, V.; Fägerlind, I. 1986. *The Design and Elaboration of the Evaluation and Monitoring Techniques for the Implementation of Educational Policies, Report Studies, S. 123.* Paris, Unesco. Division of Educational Policy and Planning.
Chinapah, V.; Miron, G. 1990. Evaluating Educational Programs: Developing Countries. In: T. Husén and T. Postlethwaite (eds.), *The International Encyclopedia of Education.* Supplementary Volume II. Oxford, Pergamon Press.

Cook, T.; Campbell, D. 1979. *Quasi-Experimentation. Design and Analysis Issues for Field Settings.* Boston, Mass., Houghton Miffin.

Couvert, R. 1979. *The Evaluation of Literacy Programmes: A Practical Guide.* Paris, Unesco.

Cronbach, L. 1951. Coefficients Alpha and the Internal Structure of Tests. *Psychometrika*, 16:297-334.

Cummings, C. et al. 1985. Practical Subjects in Kenyan Academic Secondary Schools: Background Papers. Stockholm, Swedish International Development Authority. (*Education Division Documents, No.22.*)

Dahllöf, U. 1971. *Ability Grouping, Content Validity and Curriculum Process Analysis.* New York, New York Teachers' College Press.

Daun, H. 1979. The Fishing School in Kelibia: An Evaluation of a SIDA Project, (*Report No.36.*) Stockholm, Institute of International Education, University of Stockholm.

Dave, R. 1979. *A Built-In System of Evaluation for Reform Projects and Programmes in Education.* Seminar Paper on Research and Educational Reforms, Paris, Unesco-IIEP.

El-Ghannan, M. 1980. Goals and Theories of Education: the Arab States. In: Unesco, *Educational Goals.* IBE: Studies and Surveys in Comparative Education, Paris

Fägerlind, I.; Saha, L. 1983. *Education and National Development.* Oxford, Pergamon Press.

Gopinathan, S.; Nielson, D.(eds.). *1988 Educational Research Environments in Southeast Asia.* International Development Research Centre (IDRC), Chopmen Publishers, Singapore

Grabe, S. 1983. Evaluation Manual. *Socio-Economic Studies No.6.* Paris, Unesco.

Gurugé, A. 1971. A Survey of Modern Management Techniques Applicable to Educational Administration. In: *Modern Management Techniques in Educational Administration.* New Delhi, Asian Institute of Educational Planning and Administration.

Gustafsson, I. 1987. Schools and the Transformation of Work: A Comparative Study of Four Productive Work Programmes in Southern Africa. *Studies in Comparative and International Education, No. 10,* Stockholm, Institute of International Education, University of Stockholm.

Hamadache, A.; Martin, D. 1988. *Theory and Practice of Literacy Work: Policies, Strategies and Examples.* Paris, Unesco/CODE.

Hanushek, E. A. 1979. Conceptual and Empirical Issues in the Estimation of Educational Production Functions. *Journal of Human Resources*, 14:351-88.

Harnishfeger, A.; Wiley, D. 1976. The Teaching Learning Process in Elementary Schools: a Synoptic View. *Curriculum Inquiry.* 6:5-43.

Heyneman, S.; Loxley, W. 1982. Influences on Academic Achievement across High and Low Income Countries: a Re-analysis of IEA Data. *Sociology of Education*, 55:13-21.

Hultin, M. 1986. Vocational Education in Developing Countries, *Final Draft.* Stockholm, Swedish International Development Authority.

Hunting, G. et al. 1986. *Evaluating Vocational Training Programs: A Practical Guide.* Washington D.C., World Bank.

Husén, T. 1974. *Talent, Equality and Meritocracy.* The Hague, Martinus Nijhoff.

———. et al. 1978. Teacher Training and Student Achievement in Less Developed Countries. (*World Bank Staff Working Paper, No. 310.*) Washington, D.C., World Bank.

Husén, T.; Kogan, M. (eds.). 1984. *Educational Research and Policy: How Do They Relate?* Oxford, Pergamon Press.

IIEP (International Institute for Educational Planning). 1986. *Unit on the Identification, Preparation and Evaluation of Educational Projects.* Paris, Unesco.

Johnstone, J. 1981. *Indicators of Education Systems.* Paris, Unesco-IIEP.

Karabel, J.; Halsey, A. (eds.). 1977. *Power and Ideology in Education.* New York, Oxford University Press.

Khan, Q. 1985. A Survey of the Evaluation Methods and Techniques of Educational Plans, Programmes and Projects Within the Framework of the Implementation

of Educational Policies, *Report Studies*, Paris, Division of Educational Policy and Planning, Unesco.
Kidder, H.; Judd, C. 1987. *Research Methods in Social Relations*, 5th edn. Tokyo, HRW International Editions, CBS Publishing.
Kish, L. 1965. *Survey Sampling*. New York, John Wiley.
Lauglo, J. 1985. Practical Subjects in Kenyan Academic Secondary Schools: General Report, Swedish International Development Authority, *Education Division Documents, No.20*, Stockholm
Lauglo, J.; Lillis, K. (eds.). 1988. *Vocationalizing Education: An International Perspective*. Oxford, Pergamon Press.
Levin, H. 1970. A New Model of School Effectiveness. In: *Do Teachers Make a Difference?* Washington, D.C., Office of Education, US Government Printing Office.
Lewis, E; Massad, C. 1975. *International Studies in Evaluation IV: The Teaching of English as a Foreign Language in Ten Countries*, Stockholm, Almqvist & Wiksell/New York John Wiley.
Lewy, A. (ed.). 1977. *Handbook of Curriculum Evaluation*. Paris, Unesco-IIEP.
Lillis, K. 1985. Processes of Secondary Curriculum Innovation in Kenya. *Comparative Education Review*, 29(1).
Lind, A. 1988. Adult Literacy Lessons and Promises: Mozambican Literacy Campaigns 1978-1982. *Studies in Comparative and International Education. No.12*, Stockholm, Institute of International Education, University of Stockholm.
Lundgren, U.P. 1977, *Model Analysis of Pedagogical Processes: Studies in Curriculum Theory and Cultural Reproduction*. Stockholm Institute of Education: Department of Educational Research, Stockholm
Marjoribanks, K. (ed.). 1974. *Environments for Learning*. Slough (England), NFER Publishing Company Ltd.
Makonnen, A. 1987. *Experience in Evaluative Research: The Ethiopian Literacy Campaign Evaluation*. Addis Ababa, Ministry of Education Planning and External Services.
Medley, D. 1985. Evaluating Teaching: Criteria. In: T. Husén and T. Postlethwaite (eds.), *The International Encyclopedia of Education*, Vol.3, pp. 1734-47. Oxford, Pergamon Press.
Nachmias, C.; Nachmias, D. 1987. *Research Methods in the Social Sciences: Alternative Second Edition without Statistics*. London, Edward Arnold.
Nevo, D. 1985. Evaluation, role of. In: T. Husén and T. Postlethwaite (eds.), *The International Encyclopedia of Education*, Vol. 3, pp. 1772-74. Oxford, Pergamon Press.
Niles, F. 1981. Social Class and Academic Achievement: a Third World Reinterpretation. *Comparative Education Review*, 25: 419-30.
Nunally, J. 1967. *Psychometric Theory*. New York, McGraw-Hill.
Nyagah, B. 1985. The Conditions of Industrial Educational Workshops and Equipment. In: C. Cummings et al., Practical Subjects in Kenyan Academic Secondary Schools: Background Papers, Swedish International Development Authority, *Education Division Documents, No.22*, Stockholm
Nyström, K. 1985. Schooling and Disparities: A Study of Regional Differences in Sri Lanka. *Studies in Comparative and International Education No. 9*, Stockholm, Institute of International Education, University of Stockholm.
Patton, M. 1975. Alternative Evaluation Research Paradigm. *North Dakota Study Group on Evaluation Monograph Series*. Grand Forks, University of North Dakota.
——. 1978. *Utilization-Focused Evaluation*. Beverly Hills, Calif., Sage Publications.
——. 1980. *Qualitative Evaluation Methods*. London, Sage Publications.
——. 1985. Evaluation for Utilization. In: T. Husén and T. Postlethwaite (eds.), *The International Encyclopedia of Education*, Vol. 3, pp. 1748-50. Oxford, Pergamon Press.
Peaker, G. 1975. *International Studies in Evaluation VIII: An Empirical Study of Education in Twenty-One Countries: A Technical Report*. Stockholm, Almqvist & Wiksell/New York, John Wiley.

Postlethwaite, T. N. 1984. *Monitoring and Evaluation of Educational Projects*. Hamburg, University of Hamburg.
Psacharopoulos, G. (ed.). 1980. *Information: An Essential Factor in Educational Planning and Policy*. Paris, Unesco.
Ross, K. 1987. Sample Design. *International Journal of Educational Research*, 11(1): 57-75.
Rossi, P. (ed.). 1982. *Standards for Evaluation Practice*. San Francisco, Calif., Jossey-Bass.
Rutman, L. (ed.). 1984. *Evaluation Research Methods: A Basic Guide*. Beverly Hills, Calif., Sage Publications.
Schiefelbein, E; Simmons, J. 1979. *The Determinants of School Achievement: A Review of the Research for Developing Countries*. Ottawa, International Development Research Centre (IDRC).
Shaeffer, S; Nkinyangi, J. (eds.). 1983. *Educational Research Environments in the Developing World*. Ottawa, International Development Research Centre (IDRC).
Silanda, E. 1988. Education and Regional Differences: A Study of the Nature and Causes of Educational Disparities in Zambia, *Master's Degree Studies No.2*, Stockholm, Institute of International Education, University of Stockholm.
Simmons, J.; Alexander, L. 1978. The Determinants of School Achievement: A Review of the Research. *Economic Development and Cultural Change*. Vol. 26: 341-67.
Sim Wong Kooi 1975. The Evaluation of Educational Plans. *Bulletin of the Unesco Regional Office for Education in Asia and the Pacific, No.16*. Bangkok, Unesco.
Soumelis, C. 1983. The Evolution of Educational Planning Concepts and Approaches - an Overview. In: OECD 1983, *Educational Planning: A Reappraisal*, pp.12-51. Paris, OECD.
Spaulding, S. 1985. Evaluation in Adult Education: Developing Countries. In: T. Husén and T. Postlethwaite (eds.). *The International Encyclopedia of Education*, Vol. 3, pp. 1753-57. Oxford, Pergamon Press.
Thorndike, R. 1973. *International Studies in Evaluation III: Reading Comprehension in Fifteen Countries*, Stockholm, Almqvist & Wiksell/New York, John Wiley.
Tung, K.; Chinapah, V. 1985. *Universalization of Primary Education and Literacy: Phase II - Research and Evaluation Studies*. Paris, Unesco.
Tyler, R. 1989. Evaluation for Utilization. In: T. Husén and T. Postlethwaite (eds.). *The International Encyclopedia of Education*. Supplementary Volume One, pp. 347-56, Oxford, Pergamon Press.
UNDP. (United Nations Development Programme) 1988 *Guidelines For Project Formulation and the Project Document*.
Unesco. 1982a. *From Planning to Plan Implementation: Seven Training Modules*. Bangkok, Unesco Regional Planning Office.
Unesco. 1982b. Monitoring of Literacy Programmes, Planning, Administration and Monitoring in Literacy, *Portfolio of Literacy Materials Series 2 No.1*. Bangkok
Unesco-IBE. 1986 *International Yearbook of Education: Vol.38: Primary Education on the Threshold of the Twenty-First Century*. Paris, International Bureau of Education, Unesco.
Walker, D. 1976. *International Studies in Evaluation IX: The IEA Six Subject Survey: An Empirical Study of Education in Twenty-One Countries*, Stockholm, Almqvist & Wiksell/New York, John Wiley.
Weiss, C. H. 1984. Increasing the Likelihood of Influencing Decisions. In: L. Rutman (ed.), *Evaluation Research Methods: A Basic Guide*. Beverly Hills, Calif., Sage Publications.
Wilcox, R. 1985. Simulation as a Research Technique. In: T. Husén and T. Postlethwaite (eds.). *The International Encyclopedia of Education*, Vol. 8, pp. 4565-66. Oxford, Pergamon Press.
Wolf, R. (ed.). 1987. Educational Evaluation: The State of the Field. *International Journal of Educational Research*, 11(1).
Wu Wei. 1986. Reform and Strengthen Education Research. *China Educational Science*, Beijing, Central Institute of Educational Research (CIER).

(B) SHS.89.XVII.15/A